The Catskills

The Catskills
Land in the Sky

Text by John G. Mitchell
Photographs by Charles D. Winters
Introduction by Brooks Atkinson
Preface by Senator Daniel P. Moynihan

A Studio Book   THE VIKING PRESS   New York
in association with The Catskill Center

Text printed in the United States of America by Halliday Lithograph. Color photographs printed in Japan by Dai Nippon Printing Company.

Library of Congress Cataloging in Publication Data
Mitchell, John G
   The Catskills.
   (A Studio book)
   1. Catskill Mountains—Description and travel.
I. Winters, Charles D., 1941-   II. Title.
F127.C3M57   974.7'38   77-9909
ISBN 0-670-20852-3

Contents

Illustrations: Page 1. The Catskills from the east bank of the Hudson River. 2 and 3. Foggy morning in Treadwell. 4. Blue vervain. 5. Bridge at Devil's Kitchen. 6 and 7. Looking northeast from Slide Mountain. 8. Young sparrow hawk.

Dedicated to
the Catskills of tomorrow

Acknowledgments

For much of the historical lore in this work the author gratefully acknowledges two invaluable sources: *The Catskills: From Wilderness to Woodstock* by Alf Evers, and *The Catskill Mountain House* by Ronald Van Zandt. For the rest of it, he salutes the people of the Catskills in general, and in particular Peter Borrelli of The Catskill Center, whose sense of place—and of balance—guided every aspect of this book from beginning to end.

J. M.

The Catskill Center gratefully acknowledges the A. Lindsay and Olive B. O'Connor Foundation, The J. M. Kaplan Fund, and the New York State Council on the Arts for their generous support, without which this book would not have been possible.

The Catskill Center

The Catskill Center for Conservation and Development, Inc., founded in 1969, is a private nonprofit citizens' organization which has devoted itself to the study, preservation, and protection of valuable farmlands, forests, parks, streams, and historic sites. Membership and participation in the Center are invited. Headquarters: The Catskill Center, Hobart, New York 13788.

Foreword

The Catskills were the first American wilderness, celebrated and popularized in verse and painting and in the journals of learned men long before the West was won. As such they have suffered much because of their proximity to the population centers of a growing nation. These "blue mountains," first spied by Henry Hudson from the deck of the *Half Moon*, were all too near New York City, Boston, and Philadelphia to escape their grasping influence. After an early and seamy history of land speculation and colonial land grants, the Catskills were robbed of their forests, rock, wildlife, and water. Throughout it all a hardy and stubborn people stayed on in the valleys and on the mountains, farming hardscrabble and living off the land. Though it gave little in return, they learned to love the land. But the pressure from the cities never ceased. First came steel rails, then highways. And with them came more and more people. The land became divided and divided again.

The continuing division of the land has created both diversity and disunity throughout the Catskills. It is an enormous region without, to some extent, a regional identity. One lives in Shandaken or Stamford or Livingston Manor or Windham, but seldom in the Catskills. Each place, however, is part of a whole worn by wind and water and held together in time, despite man's efforts to make of the Catskills what has already become of so many other parts of America.

It is this Catskills, that which has survived greed and destruction, that we seek to preserve; not as a park or picture postcard image,

11

but as a living landscape providing both sustenance and inspiration to man. We seek a harmony of man and nature, which comes first by being awakened to the beauty and message of nature. Marston Bates described our concern and hope for man and nature when he wrote:

> In defying nature, in destroying nature, in building an arrogantly selfish, man-centered, artificial world, I do not see how man can gain peace or freedom or joy. I have faith in man's future, faith in man as a part of nature, working with the forces that govern the forests and seas; faith in man sharing life, not destroying it.

It is our biased aim in this book to praise the Catskills and to speak in their defense. It has been said that as citizens we have this land as our inheritance to love and live upon and wisely use. This we believe and know to be the command of nature, which if dishonored diminishes the spirit of man.

PETER R. BORRELLI
Executive Director
The Catskill Center

Preface

Within sight of each other from their respective peaks, there exist the great city and the great wilderness, and they scarcely know of one another. Perhaps only those who have made the journey in its truest sense, which is to have lived in the one and then in the other, have a sense of the distance.

It is as if it were a distance of purpose, of intent. New York City from the first was cosmopolitan complex, multiple, singularly urban. Its great park in Manhattan here and there conjures up wilderness, but wholly for purposes of variety, rather as opera scenery. In the Catskills, by contrast, the land, seemingly, won't have urban things. The Catskills are just as stubbornly, persistingly, in the end triumphantly wild. The turnpikes, the mills, the railroads, the great hotels came. And went. John Mitchell's narrative in this eminently useful collaboration will tell you what Charles Winters' splendid photographs can only suggest, which is that there have been several cycles of settlement and development in the Catskills, each tenacious and dynamic in its way, but each doomed. In the end the great forest returned.

For fifteen years now (a fair part of my life, and the larger part of the childrens' lives) we have lived on an upland farm in Delaware County on the western slopes of the Catskills. We have not always *been* there, but this has been home. (Indeed, never so much as during two years of India where in the furnace of the North Indian Plain we maintained a measure of sanity by talking of the events at the farm: Would the peepers be chorusing yet? Or not until the weekend? Had the red-wing blackbirds arrived? Was the Queen Anne's Lace out? Were the foxes getting the grouse again? Was the snow too deep for the fawns? There were periods when no afternoon passed that I did not walk a bit in the mind's eye along the banks of the small stream that runs by our house, down through a deep, moss-green, water-black glade, into a tributary of the Susquehanna.) We have tried to stay on good terms with the wilderness, keeping it out of the fields, and pushing it back just a little here and there, but even that slight effort has made manifest the unequal nature of the encounter. The wildness returns.

There is history enough hereabouts, but it only reinforces this sense of the tentativeness of our tenure, our not-quite-free hold. Some years ago at Christmas my wife presented me with the *History of Delaware County, N.Y.*, published in 1880 by W. W. Munsell & Co. of New York. It is a splendid volume, magnanimously illustrated, and splendidly eclectic in its range and subject matter. There is, however, a unifying theme—the civilizing mission—that runs through the contributions of many authors. It appears in the first paragraph of the publisher's "Introductory." The region of quiescent peaks and peaceful valleys

> where one has harvested but grain or fruit for many a season . . . has been the scene of conflict with savage men, rude nature and wild beasts such as everywhere marked the redemption of the land from savagery, and its occupation by a Christian and highly civilized population.

Indian wars were still a living memory, for they lingered late in these mountains. (Into the nineteenth century, this was fought-over land.) So somehow did the memory of their complexity: Who was the savage, Joseph Brant or his foes? But by 1880 optimism was all, even as nostalgia crept in. In the old days, we learn, the Delaware County Militia boys were happier with the few pennies they got for gingerbread "than the lad of today would be with shillings to spend among the greatest variety of knickknacks." (Shillings and pence hung on in these hills, almost into our time.) The *History* recalls a certain rustic virtue: "the elect of the mountains, who sometimes marched to the rendezvous barefoot, carrying their boots and soldier clothes in a bundle. . . ." And notes what was lost:

> The wild deer lingered latest of the large animals. The writer saw one on the hills in 1843, and tasted the venison of one caught in the valley in 1845. [sic]

14

But optimism prevailed. The same writer continues:

The trout, that yielded to the liquor from the tanneries, will return now the bark is gone.

And how very true! Within years (of 1880) Theodore Gordon was inventing American fly-fishing on those incomparable Catskill streams, the Willowemoc and the Beaver Kill. And the deer, too, have returned. Not long ago on a late winter, almost spring afternoon we counted eleven on the edge of the uppermost of our meadows where the forest begins.

But this is the point. That was not where the forest began in 1880, or 1845. Beyond was pasture land going high up on the hill, part of an agricultural system—cows going up in the morning and coming down at night—which for a period had driven out the deer. But now the cows have begun to, well, fade. Instead of vast stands of hemlock, our climax forest is now mostly oak and maple. But the wilderness? The wilderness is back.

At least I know of no other term by which to describe the great fall-off of agriculture and local industry in the Catskills which has all but returned the land to forest and so many of our people to a near migrant condition, seeking work on the industrial fringes of the region, but having less and less hopeful life in the region itself. The fine farms and splendid carpenter Gothic houses of the residents of Delaware County of 1880 contrast painfully with the condition of so many of our people today.

This is more and more a region of public affluence and private squalor. Only those in government employ seem able to afford the graces of life; even its necessities, more and more, are dispensed *by* government. And by a distant government at that.

The more then might we cherish the thought of the local organizations which have taken up the cause of the Catskills. We have ever been a people alert to the rewards of such enterprise. Tocqueville noted this on his visit to the United States in 1831.

Americans of all ages, all conditions, and all dispositions constantly form associations. They have not only commercial and manufacturing companies, in which all take part, but associations of a thousand other kinds, religious, moral, serious, futile, general or restricted, enormous or diminutive. The Americans make associations to give entertainments, to found seminaries, to build inns, to construct churches, to diffuse books, to send missionaries to the antipodes; in this manner they found hospitals, prisons, and schools. If it is proposed to inculcate some truth or to foster some feeling by the encouragement of a great example, they form a society. Wherever at the head of some new undertaking you see the government of France, or a man of rank in England, in the United States you will be sure to find an association.

An association for political, commercial, or manufacturing purposes, or even for those of science and literature, is a powerful and enlightened member of the community, which cannot be disposed of at pleasure or oppressed without remonstrance, and which, by defending its own rights against the encroachments of the government, saves the common liberties of the country.

The author of the 1880 chapter on the Town of Davenport in the *History* did not fail to observe this phenomenon. In a short section of his narrative he states: "There have been three secret societies in the township. The Fugine Society was organized in 1843. During the rage for an American party there was a dark lantern lodge that claimed to Know Nothing about it. The Free Masons were also represented." From the past tense of the narrative, we must assume that none of these were active as late as 1880, and indeed were of Tocqueville's period, for, political parties aside, there came about a certain impoverishment of local organization in these mountains. All the more then do we welcome the establishment of the Catskill Center for Conservation and Development, and similar centers of informed concern about the future of this first and persisting American wilderness.

DANIEL P. MOYNIHAN
Pindars' Corners
Delaware County
April 14, 1977

Introduction

It all began irresponsibly. After a delightful summer vacation in the Adirondacks, my wife, Oriana, and I discussed the possibility of buying a vacation home. We did not particularly like the Catskills, but they are within driving distance of New York City. As a veteran camper in the White Mountains I looked down on the Catskills as commonplace, and Oriana, a native of New York City, accepted them without much enthusiasm. But she has more bounce than I do and promptly took off to investigate Durham in Greene County—the Strout Farm catalog, which was a sacred relic in her family's home, showed photographs of a farm or two that looked attractive. She has already told the story of that whimsical buying spree in *Not Only Ours*, and I shall not repeat it except to remark that it resulted in our buying a crumbling farmhouse, built about 1797, with 111 acres of farmland.

Now, nearly a half century later, we are both astonished by the naïveté with which we bought family property in a town we knew nothing about. We overlooked the fact that Durham is a community about two hundred years old with standards of its own and considerable ethical pride. In a manner of speaking, we insulted the natives by dropping in, buying one of the oldest farms, and automatically returning to the city as soon as the papers were signed. We vaguely assumed that we would live in the old house a few weeks in the summer, resting from the heedless, brilliant whirlwinds of New York City; and after a pleasant vacation we would return to the main activities of our lives—books, newspapers, libraries, the performing arts, parties.

Durham gave us more than we gave Durham. What happened to us was totally unexpected and enlightening. When we returned from the city the next spring, we were overwhelmed by the extravagant luxury of the apple, pear, and cherry blossoms and the glory and fragrance of the locust. Life was bursting out all over. Bluebirds nested in the grape trellis near the kitchen windows. The happy melodies of meadow larks, robins, orioles, and wood thrushes sweetened the morning air. Swifts were throbbing in our fireplace chimney. We realized that we were not just visiting but intruding in a place where we would have to learn how to cope with a new style of life.

Once we had invaded their privacy, people were completely hospitable and generous. Both of our next-door neighbors were separated from us by four or five intervening hayfields. Eli Campbell, who lived with his warmhearted sister, Libby, was a routine farmer who kept cows, horses, hens, geese, ducks, hogs, and one personable dog, Tipper. Eli knew everyone, talked enthusiastically, and helped me with things I could not deal with. I asked him who would cut the tall grass overwhelming our lawns. Eli did it himself. I did not realize that it would involve hitching up a mowing machine that had been stowed away since the previous summer, and I felt like an insufferable bore when he would not accept any payment.

Up the road, Clifford and Myra Hubbard ran a thriving farm. When we walked up to their home in the evening they received us not only with politeness but with cordiality. Many of my ideas were adolescent and fatuous. The Hubbards did not argue, although they obviously did not agree with me. I consulted them often about such things as people who wanted to cut our hay or plow our garden. Without denigrating anyone, they protected me from those who were charlatans, and we gradually became close friends.

In 1929 I noted in my journal: "This country life satisfies me completely, and a satisfied man is no writer." And the next October: "All through the Catskills the golds and the browns seep gloriously across the landscape. No two trees are alike. The soft loveliness of the night, the pale white of the moonlight, the soothing quiet and beauty of the country are reassuring."

In comparison with the White Mountains and the Adirondacks, the Catskills are mild. Our closest mountain, Pisgah, is 2912 feet high. Once it was a tourist attraction. In 1876, Walter Doolittle, a native of an adjoining town, built a carriage road to the summit, and a small hotel and view tower. In a single summer, fifteen hundred people came to see the view and enjoy a holiday. The buildings burned to the ground in 1925, but when we came to Durham many people regaled us with memories of visits to the mountaintop. The summit was open then; most of Pisgah was a pasture. In the early 1930s it became one of the state's tree farms. Spruce seedlings planted then have now become a forest of trees sixty and seventy feet tall, and some red pines interspersed among them have become massive towers. The trees cover the flanks and top of the mountain and cramp the view from the summit. The road is now a deeply eroded trail.

For many springs and summers I visited the forest on Pisgah two or three times a week before breakfast to look for birds and flowers. It is a storehouse of natural wealth. Last summer, when I was climbing the west slope of the mountain through the aromatic green forest, a piece of rusty barbed wire caught my ankle, reminding me that years ago cattle and sheep were pastured there. Now all that remains are a few cellar holes and capped wells, the rusty frame of a discarded mowing machine, a clump of aging apple trees, a huge and glorious lilac bush that shouts for joy every spring, and a spreading sycamore that some long-gone farmer enthusiastically planted on what was once the front lawn of his farmhouse.

We now live in Durham all through the year. I cut the grass in summer and stagger behind a snow blower in the winter. Strangers who have moved in recently look on us as old-timers. It might surprise them to learn that after nearly fifty years I still feel like an intruder when I am talking to a native. I am still a Johnny-come-lately here, in spite of the fact that the Catskills are my home and I cherish them.

In the years since we bought our house the town has changed remarkably. Many of the farms (all the small ones, I think) have gone out of business. Only those operated by the ablest and most vigorous farmers remain in use. Despite all the difficulties—new laws, new standards, new equipment, high prices—they seem to prosper. The new generation seems to want to continue the family tradition. The hay in our field has been cut regularly by neighbors who need it or value it as a salable commodity. In the days of horse-drawn machinery the annual chore of haying took a couple of months and occasionally extended into October. Now it is finished in a couple of weeks.

Some of the farms have been broken up into building lots, and many ranch-type houses have been built there by summer people. I regret the loss of the wide, calm, neighborhood feeling, and I notice that new summer inhabitants do not become personal friends as earlier ones did. That may be my fault; I should take the initiative. I regret the rapid proliferation of trailers all through the town, although I recognize that may be the only economical way to solve the housing problems of the owners. But in general, the living standards have improved remarkably.

In view of stupendous national problems, the future of our town and the Catskills is going to change. The changes that have already been accomplished will continue, and I can only hope that they will be constructive. Many serious dangers are recognizable. The natural grace and beauty of the environment may succumb to the weight of a materialistic civilization in which everything becomes standardized.

Many residents of the Catskills recognize these dangers of the future and wonder what to do about them. They, and the state legislature, which has also become concerned and is trying to establish planning guidelines, are the custodians of the future. The problems are numerous and powerful and many of them must be unpredictable. But the Catskills must not be allowed to go by default. Ways must be found for the inhabitants to earn a living without destroying the loveliness and patience of the Catskills. So far the record has been encouraging.

BROOKS ATKINSON
Durham, New York

Hooked

"I have travelled the woods for fifty-three years, and have made them my home for more than forty; and I can say that I have met but one place that was more to my liking. . . ."

"And where was that?" asked Edwards.

"Where! why up on the Cattskills. . . . There's a place in them hills that I used to climb to when I wanted to see the carryings on of the world, that would well pay any man for a barked shin or a torn moccasin. You know the Cattskills, lad; for you must have seen them on your left, as you followed the river up from York, looking as blue as a piece of clear sky, and holding the clouds on their tops. . . ."

"What see you when you get there?" asked Edwards.

"Creation," said Natty, dropping the end of his rod into the water and sweeping one hand around him in a circle: "all creation, lad."

—James Fenimore Cooper, *The Pioneers*

In the beginning, like Natty Bumppo's foil, I knew the Catskills only from the outside corner of the left eye. They seemed never so clear as a piece of sky, nor so blue. To my eye, they appeared gray, worn, shapeless, not holding the clouds but often lost in them; vaguely evoking a memory of arcane schoolboy legends and a riffle of subliminal flash cards across the scrim of my wandering mind. *Dutch,* said a card.

Kosher, said another. *Resorts . . . water . . . supply . . . forest . . . preserve . . . wild . . . forever.* And as the free associations passed, so did the Catskill Mountains, quickly on the left as we followed the river north from New York; or, more precisely, as we followed the Thomas E. Dewey Thruway from New York toward a different destination. Namely, the Adirondacks. Oh, how those glimmering forever wilder mountains of the north had a hold on me then—how almost every mountain range that I had seen had a hold on me then! The Whites of New Hampshire. The Colorado Rockies. The Medicine Bows of Wyoming. The Selkirks of Northern Idaho. But not the Catskills of New York, which I had known only from the corner of one eye and by hearsay proxy, and which served me in those days as a mere landmark, a milepost along the way to the Adirondacks.

One summer a funny thing happened on the way to the Adirondacks. I saw the Catskills with both eyes. A part of them, any way. I saw the long escarpment west of Saugerties beseiged by thunderheads at dusk. Great rapiers of lightning slashed raggedly across the mountaintop. Clouds tumbled and exploded in brilliant flickering flare-bursts that seemed to illuminate the whole western sky. Every flash gave a clear new shape to the mountain. Between flashes the mountain loomed massive and black above the Hudson Valley flatlands which even now absorbed the first fat tentative raindrops of the approaching storm. I was uneasy. I remember thinking that I could feel the mountain beyond the windows of the car, feel the pull of its presence, the force of some inexplicable gravity threatening at any moment to wrench us sideways on the rain-slick surface of the road. "It's only the downdraft from passing trucks," someone remarked from the back seat. "No," said another, "it's the wind." I said nothing. And then the mountain disappeared as a milky cloudburst engulfed us, and we drove on, Adirondacks or bust, through the pelting rain.

In the Adirondacks in those days I was a scrambler, a bagger of peaks. On the heels and in the dust of a long-legged friend, I would dedicate the precious daylight hours of every vacation to the conquest of elevations in excess of four thousand feet. Neither rain nor gale, not

22

even a deep-rooted acrophobic neurosis, could deter me from my appointed rounds of the highest summits. One a day, two a day. From Dix to Nippletop in two hours flat. It was madness. One drizzly morning as my friend sat at the breakfast table searching his guidebook for new peaks to conquer, I found myself struck by a clarity of purpose. Without apology or explanation, I announced that I was bagging no more peaks. Good grief! But what would I do with myself? I said I intended to go to the valley and learn how to fish. For a change, I would endeavor to bag trout. "You'll get hooked," said my friend. "You'll lose touch with the mountains." As it turned out, he was only half right. I got hooked, all right. But I did not lose touch with the mountains. With rod and reel I took new delight in them. And I discovered the Catskills.

Anyone who angles for trout and at the same time succumbs to a historical curiosity about the sport sooner or later *has* to discover the Catskills. They are the sacred fount of fly-fishing in America. They are where it all began, this other madness, this flailing of gin-clear pools with sparse gray hackles. And so, with scant adieus to the Adirondacks, I began to poke along the edges of the mountains I had bypassed, wetting my line in the holy waters of such fabled Catskill streams as the Esopus, the Beaverkill, the Schoharie, and the Neversink. Where the great masters once had flourished, I flailed and failed to bag even one respectable trout—a circumstance I blame on my own desultory style as much as anything else. But it did not matter, really, for each exploratory visit drew me deeper into the mountains, up the twisting two-lane roads, across the cloves, the passes, to the secret places, the special pools and riffles, the hemlock gorges, the waterfalls, the covered bridges, the somnolent streamside villages of Sundown and Branch and Cragie Clair and Chichester and West Kill and Mosquito Point; places that, in time, would come to mean far more to me than the act of depriving a fish of its right to life. I was getting hooked, all right. But not on trout.

So the region grew on me, drew on me, pulling me back even without the rod and reel, in season and out of season, the apostate Adirondacker, the Catskill convert. Hooked. Hooked on the furrowed faces of wind-chapped men in overalls at roadside diners, the bright bandanas of farm women out to fetch the morning mail, the rocking chairs on gingerbread porches, the swayback barns adrift in fields of autumn stubble, the smell of sunburnt balsam on hot afternoons, the glide of smooth water over polished stone, the raucous clamor of flocking crows, the rough texture of conglomerate on a wind-swept ledge. And more, much more.

There was a time, but a very brief one, when I believed I had arrived at a substantial understanding of the Catskills. Surely, I thought, enough miles had been logged, enough lore and wisdom absorbed from indigenous folk, for me to say, "Catskills, I know you." But, of course, I was wrong. *Know* the Catskills? How? How could one even begin to grasp all there is to know about four thousand square miles and a quarter-million diverse and independent people? How could one know the Catskills when, in the sense and the spirit of regionalism, the Catskills do not even know themselves? How could one reasonably expect, after five or ten years (or twenty, Mr. Rip Van Winkle), to return to any village or valley and find it exactly the same? Obviously, one couldn't. Autumn stubble in time succeeds to yellow birch—or mobile homes. A village briefly nourished by economic happenstance reverts to boarded windows and quiet despair. A barn collapses. A highway is rerouted. A railroad shuts down, rust on the tracks. A mountainside sheds its trees for a crop of A-frame chalets. Know the Catskills? No way. Time will not stand still for it.

A mountaineer of my acquaintance, a shin-barked fellow from the Far West, once endeavored to ascertain what exactly it was that I *saw* in the Catskills. Why, they hardly qualified as mountains, he said. Not a single summit above the tree line. Spotted all over with pastures and such. Nothing to sink a piton into. Hills, he sneered. And crawling all over with people. Why, even in the East, the Catskills were outclassed. The Smokies were woodsier, the Adirondacks wilder, the Whites of more spectacular scale. He even had praise for the vertical cliffs of the nearby Shawangunks. But the Catskills? What could they possibly offer?

Atop Cornell Mountain

Winter Hollow

"Dinosaur bones" on Giant Ledge

Winnisook Road Falls

Front door of Lexington House Hotel

Window of John Burroughs's Woodchuck Lodge, Roxbury

Lexington Post Office

Hanford Mills Museum, East Meredith

Marsh Marigold

Woodchuck

< ∧ Fritillaries

Beaverkill

Stony Clove Notch, Hunter

Pine grove, Cooper Lake

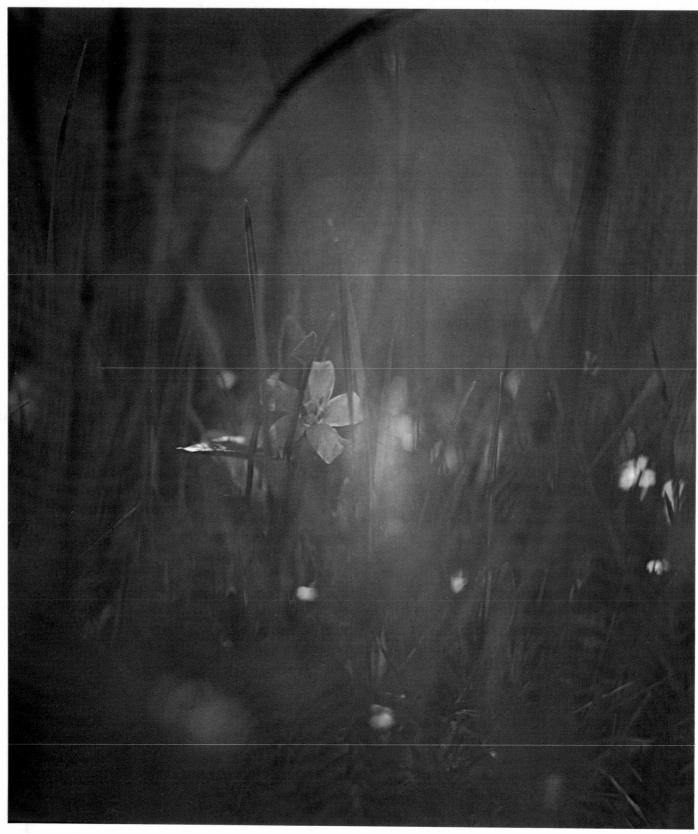

Periwinkle (Myrtle)

A familiar question, I replied, having raised it myself some time before. But now I thought I had an answer. It was not as grandiose as Natty Bumppo's. I was not about to tell this fine fellow that in the Catskills one can see "all creation." Just that one can see a good part of America—and a bit of the bad part as well. I mean the good resiliency of nature—fields grown to hardwood insurrection, cutover forests regenerating on protected lands. I mean the dreadful dissolution of nature—suburban sprawl, rechanneled streams, the squalid assumption that ownership of property precludes the stewardship of soil. To my mind, good is rural people pasturing on gingerbread porches. Bad is foreclosure and boarded windows. Good is the simple life in small communities. Bad is the fortress mentality of small communities. Good is a constitutional guarantee that some of this land shall remain forever wild. Bad is the almost certain assurance that some of these people will remain forever cash-poor. Good is the mountain country's ability to serve the big city with water for drinking and open space to recreate the city folks' souls. Bad is the city's ungrateful response: leaky faucets and weekend litter.

The mountaineer did not understand. His head was too much in the clouds. He did not like the dichotomy. He said that by my definition the Catskills were "a can of worms." I replied that a can of worms could provide a magnificent challenge. But he did not understand that either, and I think I know why. For all his years among mountains, he had never once found the time to go fishing, to drop the end of his rod in the water and catch something larger than trout.

"Two Stones to Every Dirt"

It is not easy to define the boundaries of the Catskill Mountains. I once asked an old man who lived within the shadow of Plattekill Mountain just where the Catskills began. "You keep on going," he said, "until you get to where there's two stones to every dirt. Then, b'Jesus, you're there."

—ALF EVERS,
*The Catskills: From Wilderness
to Woodstock*

Unless etymologists are mistaken, the name Catskills probably comes from an English corruption of the colonial Dutch *kat kill*. It is generally agreed that *kill* is Dutch for creek. Exactly what *kat* meant in colonial times is a matter of much dispute, some scholars skinning it as "cat," while others insist that *kat* had nothing whatsoever to do with felines but rather with "glacis," meaning the outward sloping walls of a fortification or earthwork. Either seems logical enough. The eastern encarpment of the mountain region does indeed resemble a glacis; and bobcats no doubt padded freely along the streams of the mid-Hudson valley until settlement drove them to safety at higher elevations. However logical, neither derivation is accepted by a third school of experts who contend that Catskill Creek, draining the northeast slopes of the mountains, was given its name by Henry Hudson, in honor of Jacob Cats, then the national poet of the Netherlands. No matter. Corruption of one kind or another in time bestowed on mountains and creeks such names as Kaaterskill, Katskills, Caderskill, Kauterskill, and Katzbergs, among two dozen others. Under British rule, it was fashionable to refer to the Blue Mountains, but this name was soon dropped in deference to the other Blue Mountains, the main stem of the Alleghenies. And one must not forget that the Indians, according to Henry Schoolcraft, called the mountains *Ontiora*—land in the sky. This also seems logical and corruptible. The nineteenth-century poet Henry Abbey rearranged the Schoolcraft spelling to write of:

> *The monster, Onteora,*
> *Came down in the dreadful gloom.* . . .
> *By eternal silence touched,*
> *Fell backward in a swoon,*
> *And was changed into lofty hills,*
> *The mountains of the sky.*

Yet despite the onslaught of poets and katskinners, Catskills it became. It is a fine old jolly Knickerbockerish sort of name, and it fits, which is all that anyone except an etymologist should expect.

Over the years, there has probably been as much disagreement and confusion over *what* the name fits as how it happened to arrive in our vocabulary in the first place. Ask a random stranger on the streets of Manhattan to locate the Catskills and chances are that he or she will promptly direct you to the resort nexus of Sullivan County, New York. Put the same query to a maturing flower child and you are likely to learn that the Catskills are in Woodstock. Ask a cartographic purist and you may hear about the "Blue Line," which does indeed appear on some maps to define the so-called Catskill Park. But the park itself is a confusion. Many people mistakenly believe it is one and the same as the Catskill Forest Preserve. It isn't. The park has 650,000 acres, almost two-thirds of which are privately owned. Within the park is the preserve, which encompasses the other third, the scattered state-owned tracts that, by an amendment to the state constitution, have been "forever kept as wild forest lands" since 1894. But the Blue Line is not the

Catskills *in toto*. And neither are most of the other lines, except for the Green Line, which is flung far and wide around the Catskills and thereby discredits itself with a surfeit of acres.

The Green Line appeared in 1975, the creation of the Temporary State Commission to Study the Catskills. It is a regional planner's dream, this line. It follows county boundaries neatly, except in the northeast, where it gerrymanders the suburbs of Albany. It takes in six thousand square miles, all of the Blue Line Park, Woodstock, and Sullivan County. It also takes in the cities of Oneonta, Cooperstown, and Cobleskill, which, before the commission's study, had not been generally regarded as Catskillian communities; not to mention lesser hamlets along the northern edge of the Green Line that would seem, for a variety of reasons including distance, to be more closely associated with the Mohawk Valley than the Catskill Mountains.

How, then, to define the boundaries of the Catskills, to circumscribe the physical and societal place? This is not a simple task, for while the mountains on the east and northeast rise abruptly from the Hudson Valley flats, on the north, west, and south they seem to fade away across the great Allegheny Plateau like old hunchback soldiers who will not die. Thus, if one is pressed to sketch a reasonable perimeter, there is nothing for it but to proceed in a cavalier and ruthless fashion, first getting one's bearings by the wisdom of common consent and misdemeanor plagiarism, then taking a ridgeline here, a highway there, a creek bottom, a straightedge on the map if need be, to complete the boundaries.

For the purposes of this book we shall proceed clockwise from high noon at Stamford in Delaware County. Why Stamford? Why *not* Stamford? It is a lovely old town in the shadow of Mt. Utsayantha. Looking north from Utsayantha on a clear day, one can see the old soldiers marching off toward the Mohawk Valley. So here we begin. Heading east toward three o'clock, we find nothing tangible to follow, so we must invent a straight line across the Schoharie Valley to Catskill Creek, hitting it, say, a few miles upstream from Oak Hill; then down Catskill Creek to the New York Thruway near Leeds. Now we turn south on the Thruway to Rosendale. We are committing a heresy here, I suppose. We are excluding the city of Catskill. But why include Catskill in the Catskills when, instead of looking to the mountains, Catskill is eyeball to eyeball with the Hudson River, as are Saugerties and Kingston? River towns. Excluded.

Rosendale is at four o'clock and now, blessedly, we leave the Thruway and head southeast along Rondout Creek to Napanoch, in the deep valley that separates the Catskills from the Shawangunks. From Napanoch we proceed along Route 209 to Wurtsboro, where we face our first real test, for Wurtsboro offers a number of options. The most generous option is to continue southwest along the Basher Kill and Neversink to Port Jervis on the Delaware River. The least generous—and the one sure to elicit the wrath of the Sullivan County Chamber of Commerce—is to meander northwestward from Wurtsboro, seeking the high ground that separates the Delaware River from the tributaries of the Willowemoc and Beaverkill, aiming for Hancock at the mouth of the Delaware's East Branch and thereby excluding a fair portion of Sullivan County; which is probably *un*fair, though some boundsmen insist it is the only way to go. The compromise option is to follow the Green Line along the boundary between Sullivan and Orange counties. However one chooses, we have now arrived at nine o'clock and all that remains is to get back to noon in Stamford. Some niggardly geographers at this point go ridge hopping from Hancock or Deposit to Stamford, along a height of land between the East and West Branches of the Delaware, and thereby exclude the distinctly indigenous hamlets of Walton, Delhi, and Hobart on the West Branch. This is an unforgivable outrage, so we shall go one ridgeline farther along the northwest, to the heights between the West Branch and Ouleout Creek. Thus do we return to Stamford by metes and bounds. We have circumscribed the Catskills.

Within this lopsided, potbellied, dog-eared lump of territory the mountains run generally northwest to southeast in three parallel groups. On the north and east, curving down from Black Dome and the escarpments near Windham, is the Great Wall of Manitou, drained to the southeast by the Kaaterskill and Plattekill, to the northwest by the

Schoharie. Next is the central block, distinguished by such promontories as Hunter and West Kill mountains and drained, from its south-facing slopes, by Esopus Creek and the East Branch of the Delaware. And finally, farthest south, the third group rolls from Pepacton to Ashokan Reservoir, a jumbled mass of peaks that include Slide (at 4180 feet, the highest of the Catskill), Panther, Peekamoose, and Wittenberg, among many others. Drainage on the south is to the Beaverkill, the Neversink, and Rondout Creek. So at last the Catskills are skinned, circumscribed, oriented, and drained. But how did they get here?

Once upon a time—say about four hundred million years ago, when primal amphibians were first learning to crawl on their fins—the land was not in the sky but under water. A great inland sea stretched across much of the Northeast. In New England there were mountains. They were very big mountains, far higher than those of today. Lightning slashed across the summits and rains swept down on them and rivers swelled in the valleys and carried the grit of which mountains are made to the shallows of the inland sea. The earth trembled and flexed. West of the mountains a thick alluvial fan—the deposited rubble of the New England summits—rose from the shallows and baked for a time in the bright oven of the sun. The sea receded. Now the wind and the rain struck across the exposed alluvium, the peneplain, the new Allegheny Plateau, carving it up, in the words of historian Alf Evers, "like a Thanksgiving turkey." But parts of the old bird were tough, sinewy with cross-bedded sandstones and shales, and topped with a conglomerate crust. Especially tough were the parts that would later be known as the Catskills.

All those centuries, millennia, epochs, and periods on the carving board; the Triassic and Jurassic, the Miocene and Pliocene; the frost warping, the wind buffing, the rain grinding and scouring through cycles of uplift and subsequent erosion. And in times so recent they would be only yesterday on a geologic calendar, great lobes of ice, some a mile thick, sliding down from the north to bury the bird for three hundred centuries, to scratch its head, resculpt its shoulders, and stuff its cavities with glacial drift. And finally came the great thaw, twenty thousand years ago, not even yesterday. *Voilà*. The Catskills: a hundred gently rounded peaks poised from one to three thousand feet above their stream-carved valleys; not mountains in the classic sense but rather what geologists call a "maturely dissected" plateau.

Of botanical matters, it is sometimes said that the Catskills are eclectic in their choice of forest cover. They were not always so. Indeed, after the retreat of the ice, there was no choice whatsoever, the chill climate of postglacial times virtually demanding that all cover be coniferous and boreal in the spruce-fir style of the North Woods. Thus it remains even today—but only on top, on the summits that rise above 3500 feet. Red spruce and balsam, mostly, twisted and stunted by the winds. Down from the higher summits, between 3500 and 1200 feet of elevation, the conifers give way to the stolid Allegheny Slope forest, which is characterized by sugar maple and beech and yellow birch and hemlock. And below that is the so-called Carolinian forest of oak, hickory, and chestnut (this last species is now nearly defunct, though showing some signs of a comeback); a southern forest, if you will, favored by maritime air wafting up the trench of the Hudson Valley. Here and there at various elevations, according to the disposition of the soil and the direction of the exposure, are ironwood, basswood, ash, aspen, white pine, and white birch. Not to mention the rich understory of shrubs, herbs, forbs, grasses, and wildflowers that in almost any watershed would likely include Dutchman's-breeches, squirrel corn, foamflower, bloodroot, trout lily, trillium, bellwort, chickweed, hemp nettle, rib grass, chicory, sow thistle, daisy fleabane, pigweed, harebell, water chinquapin, high-bush blueberry, and poison ivy, among others.

As to what extent the postglacial forests of the Catskills harbored Pleistocene shaggies, the record is scant. No doubt the mountains reverberated to the yowls and yawps of many of that period's noblest beasts—dire wolves, possibly, and cave bears, and giant stalking *kats* of one kind or another. But such specimens, alas, were not long for this world under any conditions; nor were some of their tamer successors long for the Catskills. Barely two centuries after Henry Hudson's voyage of discovery up the river that now bears his name, moose, elk, cougar, and timber wolf were gone forever from the land in the sky.

Among the notable remaining survivors of human settlement are the white-tailed deer, the black bear, and the bobcat. Deer are seemingly ubiquitous in the Catskills nowadays, notwithstanding the vicissitudes of winter weather, the lack of browse in maturing forests, and the seasonal presence of thousands of latter-day Leatherstockings who happily fulfill the function of cougars and wolves in the predatory niche. Bear are less populous and there is some concern that their numbers are declining yearly. Bobcat are so precious few, and so vulnerable to trapping, that future etymologists may think themselves justified in taking the word Catskill at face value—no Dutch, just the literal English. As for other indigenous species, there are mink, otter, beaver, raccoons, porcupines, skunks, woodchucks, hares, squirrels, mice, and voles. There are hawks and owls and buzzards, waterfowl, various birds of forest and meadow. There are lizards and toads and frogs and snakes, including the copperhead and the timber rattler. And in the waters there are bullheads and suckers and pike and bass and trout, for which latter species one must thank not nature but the hatchery managers of the New York State Department of Environmental Conservation. And finally, since the category is *survivors*, there are people, *Homo sapiens*, men, women, and children. We must not forget the people of the Catskills, as many people who are not of the Catskills so often do.

The human imprint is scuffed deeply in these mountains—more deeply, possibly, than in any other montane region of the United States. For this, one should neither thank nor blame the aboriginal peoples; their scuffing was light and inconsequential, almost without a trace but for a cornfield here and there on the lower slopes. In the manner of most pre-Columbian Indians who lived within eyeshot of high country, the Algonkian-speaking tribes of the Hudson Valley, the Iroquois to the northwest, and the Leni-Lenape to the west and south viewed the Ontiora as a sacred and ominous place: fine for hunting and berrying in hard times, perhaps, unavoidably traversable in the honored rites of making war on each other, but surely not as homeland for putting down roots. The Europeans who followed in the wake of Hudson's good ship *Half Moon* saw the mountains in a different light. They were not quite ready to *live* in the mountains, but they were more than willing to scramble about them in search of silver and gold. They searched in vain. In any event, beaver pelts soon usurped precious metals in the expansionist dreams of New Netherlands. Forts were established along the Hudson. By 1655, small settlements were secured at Catskill, Kingston, and Hurley. Hardy inquisitive folk began to mosey inland to the Esopus and Neversink valleys. From Albany, others followed the Mohawk River to the Schoharie, then turned south along that stream to the mountains. Dutch patroons in 1680 were plowing the rich Rondout bottom lands, and traders were ensconced on the banks of the Delaware. Considering the period, the logistics, and the off-again-on-again hostilities between English and Dutch, it was a fast piece of work. The colonists of Massachusetts had barely found their way to the mountains of New Hampshire. Virginians had not yet breached the Appalachian wall. Yet here in New York, as New Netherlands came to be known under English rule, the Old World culture already encircled the Catskills. And people were not only eager to exploit the mountains. Now they were ready to live in them.

Settlements within the Catskills proliferated after the Revolution. People were on the move. In particular, New England people were on the move, bone-weary of tilling their flinty hills and filled with hopes for a new life in the western territories. Thousands of Connecticut Yankees ferried across the Hudson, near Catskill, to begin the long overland journey west. Not all of them made it. Like erosional grit come to settle in the shallows of a Paleozoic sea, the poorest of the emigrants dropped from the wagon trains and fanned out through the valleys of the northern Catskills. Even today, in such distinctly Yankee villages as Windham and Durham, it is said that the country roundabout was originally settled because some people didn't have a good enough horse to get to Ohio.

There were better reasons for dropping out and staying a while in the Catskills. At various times and places over the next century and a half there were forests to be felled, hides to be tanned, stone to be quarried, resorts to be built. Industries flourished and failed, as did some of the villages. A canal linking the Hudson to the Delaware opened the southern Catskills to lively commerce in 1828. A railroad was punched through the mountains from Kingston to Stamford in 1872. Gentlemen in frock coats and ladies with white parasols were coming all the way from New York City to contemplate Nature at the vertigo lip of Kaaterskill Falls. Bohemians were moving to Woodstock. Borscht was simmering in the boardinghouses of Liberty and Monticello. Cows were outnumbering white-tailed deer in the meadows of Delaware County. And the Age of Aquarius was on its way—not via Woodstock, which grudgingly lent the great swinging festival of 1969 its name, but in a Sullivan County alfalfa field near Bethel, some sixty miles away.

Through all of its ups and downs, the Catskill region has been a place of startling contrasts. Rich and poor, castles and shacks. Scenic splendors, squalid eyesores. Forever wild, forever tamed. And at a time of the most rapacious exploitation, as the mountains were stripped of their hemlocks and fractured into paving stones for the sidewalks of New York, what else was abroad in this land in the sky? Why, nothing less than Romance with an uppercase *R*, the birth of a movement, a demand so passionate for inspiration and art and unfettered natural things that it would soon sweep from the Great Wall of Manitou to the Pacific palisades, then back again, somewhat reformed and deformed, to the alfalfa shores of Aquarius itself.

Both perspectives prevail. There are Romantics who, for the sake of their own free pasturing in wild Catskill places, would wish away everything else that the Catskills represent—the alfalfa, the corn, the cows, the lumber yards, the roads, the resorts, the villages; yes, even the people in the castles, the shacks, and the boardinghouses. Away with everything but the mountain trails, and possibly a lean-to here and there along the way to keep their sleeping bags dry when lightning streaks across the mountaintops. And at the other extreme are unromantic people. The forever-tamers. Chips off the old hemlock stump-skinners. The people who keep coming up with one more scheme to invade the forest preserve, to impound and divert the mountains' waters, to quarry big-city energy at small-town expense, to inspire the rural valleys with suburban sprawl and plastic recreations. And somewhere in between, I suspect, are the *other* people, the mountain people whose feeling for unfettered country is no less passionate than that of my friends, the Romantics, but who know nonetheless that the mountains must give them something in addition to greenery and fresh air. Namely, a living.

Geddy Sveikauskas, editor of the *Woodstock Times,* once observed that there are "two Catskills, representing in their uneasy alliance a mockery of the ideal of intelligent interaction between man and his environment." Sveikauskas, of course, was referring to the Catskills represented by the forest preserve and the Catskills represented by the private ownership of land, where virtually "anything still goes much as it has for the past century and a half." One keeps hoping that Sveikauskas, however right he was about the region's past and present, will be proven wrong about its future. One keeps hoping for a Third Catskills, where man and nature are in balance and at peace.

Philistines and Philosophers

And in looking over the yet uncultivated scene, the mind's eye may
see far into futurity. Where the wolf roams, the plough shall glisten;
on the gray crags shall rise temple and tower—mighty deeds shall
be done in the now pathless wilderness; and poets yet unborn shall
sanctify the soil.

—Thomas Cole,
Essay on American Scenery

Throughout the chronicle of Catskill deeds both mighty and miscreant,
one special place turns up again and again, eminent above all others. It
is as if the Great Manitou itself, or possibly the monster Onteora, had
long ago decreed that there must be a geomorphic cornerstake for hitching up the strange and awesome plow horses of history. It is a small
piece of country, this place, hardly one one-thousandth of the 4000-
square-mile whole. It embraces no seat of governmental power, sup-
ports no venerable settlement to speak of, and lacks, like the mountain
region of which it is the touchstone, the official stamp of specificity
on any map. Today, but for a twisting road or two, a state campground,
and a lacework of foot trails through the woods, the place is much
the same as it must have been when the chronicle began. A bit worn,
perhaps; defrocked of its ancient stands of pine and balsam; its ledges
here and there defaced with the engraved initials of passing pilgrims.
Yet much the same nonetheless in the way that water still plunges
down the steep cleft of the Kaaterskill Clove, the way North and South

lakes still nestle behind the rim of the escarpment, which likewise takes a sudden plunge, 1600 feet to the flats below.

Not far from the southern lake, at the edge of the precipice, is an open field, a plateau grown to wild grasses and berry thickets. People once called this part of the place the Pine Orchard. From the orchard's overhanging ledges, it was said that one could see all of creation. Actually, one could see only as far as the Taconic Mountains across the Hudson River, but in the time of frock coats and white parasols, that was creation enough. Curious things happened in the Pine Orchard. Young women swooned at the view and strong men wrote poetry by candlelight. A temple arose, all white and gleaming in the morning sun. For a hundred years people from Boston, New York, and Philadelphia, and presidents from Washington, came to genuflect at the escarpment's edge. Then changing fashions, not to mention the discovery that creation is larger than folks first thought, brought disuse to the great white temple. It is gone now, commemorated by a bronze placque on the spot. But the spirit of what it stood for haunts the Pine Orchard yet.

Long before men came to the escarpment to worship nature, other forces were at play in the high fields of the lord—the lord being one Johannis Hardenbergh of Kingston. This was at a period in our history when swooning and poetry were not allowed. Such good Christian folk as Hardenbergh and company were expected to be practical and acquisitive. Whosoever took the time to contemplate a certain landscape did so not to measure its capacity for providing inspiration but to ascertain by metes and bounds its capacity for turning profits. The record fails to indicate whether Johannis Hardenbergh ever stalked across the mountaintop between South Lake and Kaaterskill Falls. But no doubt his surveyors did, for early records show that a point barely a stone's throw from the Pine Orchard became fixed as the northeast corner of one of the most remarkable private landholdings ever assembled in colonial North America. The Great Hardenbergh Patent, they called it. Like the temple in the Pine Orchard, the patent is gone now, sliced into a thousand parcels and claims. But it is not forgotten. In fact, more than a few Catskill people still speak of the Hardenbergh Patent as though it were the fountainhead of all the greed and power-grabbing the mountains have witnessed since chroniclers started keeping score of human chicanery.

Johannis Hardenbergh may not have had much use for poetry, but in matters of business he surely had a shrewd way with words. In 1706 he presented to Lord Cornbury, cousin of Queen Anne of England and governor of New York, a petition requesting permission for himself and seven partners to settle a "small tract" of vacant and unappropriated land in the County of Ulster. Cornbury had scant regard for the value of lands along the upper Hudson, and even less for the "Blue" mountains. He would earn his place in history mainly by parading on the ramparts of Fort Anne in women's clothing, an antic which amused almost everyone except his spouse, Lady Katherine. In any event, female impersonation was not so close to Cornbury's heart that he could not recognize a serious proposition when he saw one. The Ulster tract was hilly and rocky, Hardenbergh had assured him, and was "lawfully" purchased from the Indians. So what was there to lose? It was only a small tract; at most sixteen thousand acres, inasmuch as the law limited land-grant ownership to two thousand acres per person. Or so it was said. Thus, in April 1708, Cornbury granted the patent to Johannis Hardenbergh and his seven mostly silent partners and soon thereafter departed for England. It was a wise move by the petticoat governor, for all hell would break loose among the land-hungry poor of Ulster County when they discovered that Hardenbergh's *small* tract actually stretched from Kaaterskill Clove to the East Branch of the Delaware River, a veritable empire of 1.5 million acres.

Later, the disgruntled would be hard pressed to explain how Johannis Hardenbergh had secured so great a chunk of the mountains. One theory which prevailed for a while held the patent to be Queen Anne's reward to Johannis for valor at the Battle of Blenheim. But how could that be when there were people who could swear that Hardenbergh had never been to Blenheim, much less in battle? Another explanation has it that the original patent was in fact larger than 1.5

million acres, and all because of a singular error. "Hardenbergh asked for two thousand acres like he had a right to," a Margaretville man told historian Alf Evers. "But some dumb cluck of a clerk over there in England copied things wrong and made it two million instead. . . ."

However fortuitous the acquisition, defending the patent from squatters and counterclaimants was no easy task. Hardenbergh personally gave thirty years of his life to it, afield and in court. Boundaries were squiggled here and whiplashed there. His agents were harassed on their appointed rounds. Among the troublemakers were Delaware Indians. The Delawares had been warned by the Mohawks against selling land to the white-eyes. But the land had been sold for less than a song, and now the Delawares were fearful that the Mohawks would hunt them like deer. The Delawares kept sharp eyes on Hardenbergh's surveyors. When the surveyors laid a line of rock cairns to demarcate a boundary on the banks of the East Branch, the Delawares followed at a discreet distance and tumbled the cairns into the river.

Meanwhile, many of Johannis's original partners had dropped from sight. In time, so did Johannis, but not before a full third of the patent was purchased by Robert Livingston, whose heirs and descendants would soon rival the Hardenberghs for numerical supremacy, if nothing else. One Livingston in-law of note was William Alexander, the Earl of Stirling. Chronically in debt, the earl came up with the dandy idea of holding a lottery on portions of his Great Patent lots, including a tract running back from the top of the Kaaterskill Clove. The idea appealed to Colonel George Washington of Mt. Vernon, Virginia, who, in 1772, purchased six of Stirling's lottery tickets by mail. Washington patiently waited three years for the drawing, and two of the winning tickets were his. But before the delighted gambler from Virginia could take title to his winnings in the Catskills, the lottery was declared null and void. The lots had been mortgaged to pay Stirling's debts. Washington no doubt would have sought redress but for the fact that he was now preoccupied with a war for independence; as was Lord Stirling, who served as an officer in the New Jersey militia and died with his boots on, of gout.

The American Revolution split the people of the Catskills. For the most part, the landed gentry—Hardenberghs and Livingstons and others—threw their support behind the Continental Congress. But many of their tenant farmers and other have-nots throughout the region took the Tory cause and pledged allegiance to the King. Not that they greatly admired the King; they simply detested their landlords. And what with Joseph Brant and his Iroquois scalpers skulking around the northern edge of the mountains, and raiding parties from Fort Niagara swooping down through the Kaaterskill Clove to burn and pillage the valley settlements, it seemed only prudent to be an ally of the Crown. Saving one's scalp, however, was not always the overriding motive. Should General Washington prevail, it was reasoned, Catskill tenants in all likelihood would continue to be oppressed by the same feudal manor system that had installed Johannis Hardenbergh as lord of the mountains. Yet here were the King's own agents promising a hundred acres to every man who rallied to the Crown. One can only guess to what extent such promises might have been kept had the tide of war turned the British way. Needless to say, it didn't. Washington prevailed, as did the feudal system.

Among the most colorful perpetuators of the system was a Hardenbergh heir, one Gerardus by name, alias Gross, which suited him better. According to Catskill historian James E. Quinlan, Gross Hardenbergh "feared neither man nor beast and had little respect for God or the devil." Into the Neversink Valley in the early 1800s he rode, a raunchy and abusive landlord demanding of the settlers there either eviction or rent. By some accounts, old Gross preferred the pleasures of eviction. In one instance, he is said to have dragged a settler's wife from her home "by the hair on her head." The woman died shortly thereafter. In time, so did Gross, shot in the back and knocked clean off his horse. The settlers broke out celebratory jugs and danced at his funeral. But the legacy of the Great Hardenbergh Patent would not die so quickly. In 1839, the slogan "Down with rents!" echoed through the mountains. Hardscrabble tenant farmers in sheepskin masks fell upon sheriff's deputies sent to harry them. It started with tar and feathers. It ended in blood. Yet even blood might not have halted the long and bitter strug-

Sugaring time

Stone wall

< Twin Mountain

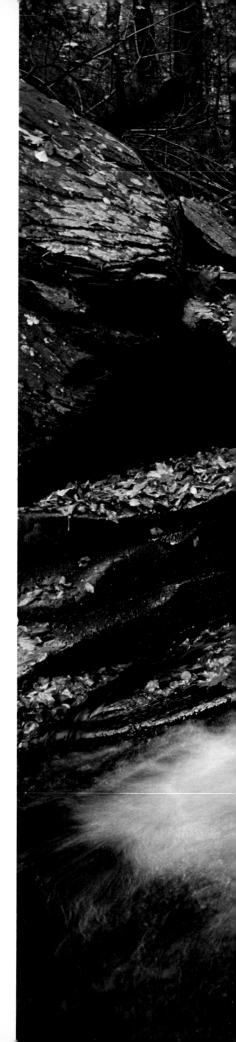

Ouleout Creek >

Fall Clove Hollow >

gle for land if owning land had remained the only means of subsistence in the Catskills. In the 1800s, however, a man had other options. Industry had arrived at last in the mountains.

By 1840, America was emerging from its first great depression. Business was especially brisk in the Catskills, with an abundance of water to spin wheels and proximity to cheap transportation on the Hudson. Craftsmen were producing everything from red-shale paints to clocks and church bells. Along the lower thirty miles of Catskill Creek, a person could count twenty-six sawmills, sixteen grist mills, ten tanneries, one brewery and a woolens factory. In a single year, from the wharves of the town of Catskill alone, Hudson River sloops carried away a quarter-million sides of shoe leather and three million board feet of lumber.

Lumber was only the frosting on the cake. At various times and places, high in the evergreen peaks and low in deciduous valleys, the richly variegated Catskill forest was rendered into bits and pieces. White pines were felled for the shipbuilders of Philadelphia, the mast-like trunks lashed together in rafts and floated down the Delaware. White ash were taken for the makers of oars and ax handles. Maple, for gunstocks and bedsteads. Into the mills went oak, birch, cherry, and spruce logs; out of the mills came the building blocks for butter paddles and barrel staves, coffins and candlesticks, porch pillars and billy clubs, shingles and shaving boxes and firkins and rocking chairs. Other trees of various species found their way to the charcoal kilns of the Esopus Valley, to the brickyards of the Hudson (as fuel), and to the acid factories of Sullivan and Delaware counties, where, toward the end of the century, wood fibers would be reduced to alcohol for varnishes, acetate for dyes, and nitrous cellulose for explosives. Earlier, at North Lake near the fabled Pine Orchard, one enterprising gentleman proceeded to ferment the essence of spruce for a popular beverage called spruce beer. Teetotalers found it slightly intoxicating. Before too many flagons went down the hatch, the spruces of North Lake had been boiled away into thin air and hiccups. Next to disappear from the orchard's environs was the balsam. For years, the young of this fragrant fir had been plucked from the escarpment, roots and all, and trundled off to the ornamental tidewater gardens of rich folk. By 1850, nary a specimen could be found for digging near the Pine Orchard. This was about the time that the Christmas tree came into its own in America. The balsam was a splendid yuletide candidate. In the Catskills, fine stands of the fir still remained within reasonable access of the rights-of-way of budding railroads. So much for the balsam, which rapidly disappeared by the carload.

And what of the hemlock? People were walking on hemlock, or wearing hemlock, in a manner of speaking. The hemlock grew to tremendous dimensions in the dark mossy cloves and gorges of the Catskills—more than a hundred feet tall and four to five feet in diameter. There were boards and billies and butter paddles galore in a mountain hemlock, but few were taken for such purposes. The hemlocks were taken for their bark, skinned and peeled for the tannin in the bark, which could turn a cowhide into leather red as the setting sun. As for the wood of the hemlock, it was left to rot, in the words of one Kingston chronicler, "like the bleaching bones of some army of giants fallen in mighty combat upon the hillsides."

The tanlords reigned for half a century. One of the first was William Edwards, who opened his New York Tannery at Hunter on the Schoharie in 1817. It was the largest structure the Catskills had ever seen, or would see for quite a while: four great chimneys presiding over a barn the length of a football field, the vats below and the smoke above. Then along came one Zadock Pratt, founder of Prattsville, the "gem of the Catskills." Pratt soon laid waste to the hemlocks of the Batavia Kill and filled his own vats with hides from Honduras and Argentina. In his definitive history, *The Catskills: From Wilderness to Woodstock*, Alf Evers describes the tannery craze that would turn this region into the leather capital of America:

In the Kaaterskill Clove, along the Sawkill, the Bataviakill, the Esopus—wherever pure water tumbled down mossy ledges and hemlock trees grew within reach of a road to the Hudson—new tanneries sprang into life. . . . Travelers seeking romantic thrills among the Catskills soon met long lines of wagons laden with stinking hides destined for mountain tanneries. Flies buzzed around the wagons. . . . Those who visited the Catskills in order to see its great primeval forests sometimes saw instead vast mountainsides and hollows covered with bleaching trunks which a long dry spell would convert into fire-blackened wastes. . . . As the mountain cover of matted roots and decaying leaves and branches burned out here and there, the very earth of the Catskills was migrating to the valleys and the sea below. . . .

So the tanlords, like the landlords before them, prospered and flourished while the mountains went down to the sea in slips. The Civil War, it was said, was fought in boots manufactured from Catskill leather. And then came the bust. One by one, the tanners looked to the ravaged mountains and saw that they had barked themselves right out of business. Except in the wildest, most inaccessible gorges, the great stands of hemlock were gone.

Another rough-and-tumble industry that would scar the mountains in the nineteenth century was the quarrying of bluestone, a hard, handsome, fast-drying relic of Late Devonian vintage. Before 1840, Catskill bluestone had been mined and finished mostly for local uses, for chimneys and hog troughs and smokehouses and cellar walls. But by mid-century, the stone had found a new and profitable market place in New York City, where people were beginning to demand something better to walk on than rough-hewn planks and uneven bricks. Soon, wagonloads of blue-gray slabs were rolling down the Esopus Valley from a hundred mountain quarries, destined for the sidewalks and plazas of New York. Visitors to the burgeoning city found the bluestone to their liking, and word spread fast. If New York could trip the light fantastic on such fabulous flagging, then why not Baltimore and Charleston, Havana and San Francisco? And with that, a hundred more quarries were carved into the ancient slopes, and the stone came out under clouds of a choking dust that powdered the forest for miles around and settled like paste on the sweating backs of the Irish immigrant laborers. Intensive quarrying no doubt would have continued into the present century but for the happenstance that innovative industries were springing up across the country. Unlike the tanlords, who were forced out of business by their own zealous excess, the bluestone quarriers finally went under because their product could not compete with a tough and inexpensive newcomer called Portland cement.

Through all the barking and blasting of the 1800s, most of the mountain people were content to perceive the physical defeat of the land as a manifestation of spiritual victory—a kingdom come and deliverance from evil, amen. Surely, many were glad to have work at whatever expense to the resource, but the motive philosophy went deeper than that, down into the potting soil of inherited beliefs and Old-World traditions first sown in America by Pilgrim and Puritan and Palatine and Patroon. "What is not useful is vicious," old Cotton Mather had whined from his pulpit in the seventeenth century. Two hundred years later, most Americans agreed—and some do still.

In 1815, the Reverend Timothy Dwight, president of Yale College, stood at the brink of the Kaaterskill Clove and proclaimed it resembled a "solitary bye-path to the nether world"—the nether world in Dwight's book being not the Hudson Valley but the satanic bowels of *Paradise Lost*. Some twenty-five years later, Charles Lanman, an associate of Daniel Webster, would report that Stony Clove (between Phoenicia and Hunter) was "the most awful corner of the world that I have ever seen," a place not unlike "the valley of the shadow of death." The clove would indeed be an awful and moribund place after the son of tanlord William Edwards finished making its hemlocks useful. But when Lanman saw it, the forest was still luxuriantly intact. Obviously, Lanman was expressing the common aversion of his day for wild, rocky, deep-shaded, uncultivated country. Devil's country, it was. Why, a man could hardly turn a corner anywhere in the Catskills without running smack up against old Lucifer himself. Especially in the dark of the cloves. Thus did the antinature bias of olden days transform itself into a Stygian mythology, and the myths into place names that prevail even today. In the vicinity of Plattekill Clove, for example, one can picnic in the Devil's Kitchen, hike the Devil's Path, and then cool off under Hell Falls. In Stony Clove is the Devil's Tombstone and a crumbling ledge known as the Devil's Pulpit, where the poor ubiquitous fellow no doubt conducts druidic services every Sunday morning before retiring to his nearby grave.

For all the blather and brimstone, by the early 1800s a few Americans were beginning to dissent from the gospel according to Mather. The frontier was beyond them now, across the Alleghenies. The Mohawks had buried their hatchets. Wolves and wildcats were on the run. Life was getting easier, safer, more settled. A man with some money was a man with some leisure. There were places to go and sights to see. A Timothy Dwight could go to the Catskills and see hell at the bottom of an abyss. But a Fenimore Cooper could go to the same spot and see all of creation. For a while yet, American seaboard society would continue to produce a hundred Dwights for every Cooper. Still, the Coopers would be heard. Their views would not shake the mountains as sharply as the thunder of a bluestone blasting charge. They would simply leave marks on the human mind—marks that would endure for generations after the scars of the quarries and clearcuts were gone.

Fenimore Cooper was by no means the first of the romantic pioneers to explore the softer side of the mountains. By some accounts, the original pathfinders were probably John and William Bartram, the Philadelphia botanists commissioned in the middle years of the 1700s to collect wild seeds and specimen trees for the formal gardens of England. Botanizing took the Bartrams far afield, to the Shenandoah Valley, the mountains of Carolina, the swamps of Florida. John, father of William, also journeyed on a number of occasions to the Catskills, the summits of which were then covered with a kind of tree much in demand among gardeners abroad. The coveted specimen was the balsam, the Balm of Gilead fir, as people called it; and Bartram knew a place in the mountains where the fir grew in profusion. British landscape gardeners were also much taken with the idea of replicating waterfalls; and Bartram knew of one in the Catskills whose splendors were beyond imagining (and beyond replicating, too, for that matter). In 1753, accompanied by fourteen-year-old William, he set out from Philadelphia to render a full account of Kaaterskill Falls and to collect balsam seeds in the Pine Orchard.

William Bartram would remember that journey and write of it later in his widely acclaimed *Travels*, published in Philadelphia in 1791. The account would be brief. It would not elaborate on the expedition's tactical failure, the scarcity of seeds to be found atop the escarpment, or his father's raging fever. It would describe instead an encounter with a rattlesnake in a "shady vale" near the Pine Orchard. The account would be read by the likes of William Wordsworth and Samuel T. Coleridge. Bartram in time would be hailed as the first American writer to deal seriously with the American wilderness. In all likelihood, he was also the first to deal, albeit briefly, with the Catskills.

Now Romance was in the air. By 1819, the path that the Bartrams had followed to the Pine Orchard was beginning to show some venerable ruts. So numerous were the pilgrims come to gaze from "the awful precipice of graywacke," as one gazetteer described the orchard, that a refreshment stand was installed on the spot to profit by their presence. This was also the year of a great publishing event, the appearance of Washington Irving's *The Sketch Book of Geoffrey Crayon, Gent.* Irving had been no closer to the Catskills than the deck of a passing Hudson riverboat, but he had studied the mountains sufficiently to be able to feature them as the setting of the *Sketch Book*'s most memorable tale, as the haunt of one legendary character named Rip Van Winkle. Rip and his Catskills took the reading public by storm. And though Irving had purposely avoided any specific reference as to where in the mountains Rip's adventure might have transpired, some readers fixed on the precincts of Kaaterskill Falls and promptly hastened there in hopes of corroborating their suspicions. The search for Rip's spoor was at its height in 1823, a year of two more great events. One was publication of Cooper's *Pioneers,* in which Natty Bumppo holds forth on creation as seen from the Pine Orchard. The other was construction in the Pine Orchard of a resort hotel that would soon dominate the entire eastern escarpment and preside there as a landmark—as *the* Catskill landmark, some said—for 139 years.

Resorts were a relatively new phenomenon in America in the early 1800s. The resort in the Pine Orchard, the Catskill Mountain House, instantly took its place among the most fashionable, vying with the spas of Saratoga and Niagara for the honor of summering the rich and famous of the day. The rich and the famous were deeply grateful. Summer had become a nightmare in the bustling seaboard cities. There was a certain aroma of sweat and disease. Dyspnea and tuberculosis were rampant. Couples retired to the sound of wheezing on the other side of the bedroom wall. Those who could afford the time and expense fled to the country, seeking relief in the salubrious air. And the higher the elevation, the better. The highest was the Mountain House. No matter that the orchard at times was shrouded in morning fog or afternoon cloud. No matter that, promenading in front of the great hotel, a visitor could sometimes detect on the prevailing westerlies the faint aroma of hemlock bark boiling in the tanneries nearby. No matter the arduous journey, though it involved being rattled about inside one of Erastus Beach's rickety stages, from the village of Catskill on the river up the dusty Little Delaware Turnpike to South Lake. However discomforting, these were small inconveniences. And even if the air *wasn't* always perfect, well—one could inhale Romance.

Among the earliest visitors to the Mountain House were a former vice-president, Aaron Burr; a governor of New York, DeWitt Clinton; and an unknown painter named Thomas Cole. Cole arrived with his sketch pads in 1825 and proceeded to break all the rules of conventional art. No clinical portraits and pastorals for this young man. Cole was caught up in the wilderness, in the Gothic crags and cloves of the Great Wall of Manitou, in landscapes "clotted by dark and tangled woods," in emotions stirred by "the silent energy of nature." Returning to his city garret, Cole transferred his sketches to canvas, and the paintings found eager buyers as fast as he could turn them out. They also found imitators. Before long, other artists were scrambling out of the Mountain House woodwork to render the mountains in oil. Cole himself regarded the hotel in the Pine Orchard as an intrusion on the wild scenery, and for many years refused to acknowledge its presence on canvas. His followers, the masters of the so-called Hudson River School, which Cole is credited with founding, were somewhat less finicky.

Thomas Cole was a magnet to creative talent. Among associates drawn by him to the Catskills was the poet William Cullen Bryant. Cole and Bryant explored the dark and tangled woods, climbed the crags, and shared each other's exuberance for the wilderness aesthetic. Possibly one of the finest paintings of the period—a large oil by Asher B. Durand, entitled *Kindred Spirits*—shows Cole and Bryant standing together in conversation on a rock ledge in Kaaterskill Clove. Cole is pointing his cane toward the top of the fabled falls.

With the works of Cooper, Irving, Bryant, Cole, and Durand calling attention to the wonders of the eastern Catskills, the success of the Mountain House was virtually assured. The modest hostel of ten private rooms and two small dormitories soon grew to sixty rooms and a grand ballroom. Cots were put up in the hallways to accommodate the overflow of guests; but even cots were not enough, and some visitors had to camp outdoors under their carriages. In 1846, Charles Beach of the stagecoach clan took title to the property and enlarged the hotel again, remodeling the facade in the Greek Revival style with thirteen Corinthian columns and a portico nearly one hundred and forty feet long. By the 1880s, after a succession of further additions, Beach's hotel could accommodate four hundred overnight guests and feed five hundred at one sitting. The fare was simple but expensive. People sat at long tables, as in a feudal banquet hall. On Sundays there were sacred rituals and sermons; no one dared to play cards. Guests arose from bed in the dark in order to contemplate the sunrise from the edge of the cliff. Jenny Lind sang at the piano. The Otis Elevating Railroad arrived in 1892. It was funicular. It hauled people straight up the Great Wall of Manitou. Now the Pine Orchard was only three and a half hours from Manhattan. This was good news for Manhattan. But for the Pine Orchard and the Catskill Mountain House, it was something else.

Coming Up Less

Faded photographs taken only forty years ago in the Esopus Valley reveal whole communities that are today all but invisible from their surrounding heights. . . . Miles of railroad tracks lie rusting along river valleys . . . stations lie abandoned in the woods. . . . Old iron gates hang sagging on their hinges, leading nowhere, mute symbols of past opulence, now hidden by the forest. . . . [An] era of human culture is now coming to an end and the mountains are returning full cycle to the first condition of their primeval past.

—Roland Van Zandt,
The Catskill Mountain House

Southeast of the Pine Orchard some fifteen miles as the crow might fly—across the Schoharie and over the Devil's Tombstone in Stony Clove and down the winding ribbon of Chichester Creek to its confluence with the Esopus—is the town of Phoenicia, New York. Like so many other Catskill communities, Phoenicia has staked its existence on tourism and recreation for a very long time. Tanners put the town on the map in the mid-1800s. Tourists have kept it there ever since. In the beginning, the old Ulster and Delaware Railroad carried them up the long grade from Kingston and deposited them a skip and a jump from the front door of the elegant grand-style Tremper House. Later there were boardinghouses and automobiles. Fishermen and hunters came seasonally and by the thousands. In the winter, skiers stopped over on their way to the slopes at Hunter and Belleayre. Good times were had by all, including the village's innkeepers and restaurateurs. Times have changed. The mood today is melancholy in Phoenicia. Tourism in the Catskills is on the skids.

In my own Esopus angling days, Phoenicia had served as the preferred base camp and supply depot for sorties along all the streams of the central Catskills. There was a small hotel on Main Street where one could generally find a solicitous bartender knowledgeable in remedies for cold feet and dry throats. And in the same block, the Brothers Volkert presided over a rod and gun ship filled with the splendid smells of pipe tobacco and Neatsfoot oil. It was a fine place to hang out when the fish weren't biting, which for me was almost always. This was about 1965, I think. Then other streams in other parts of the mountains lured me away from Phoenicia. Route 28 was widened and otherwise improved in such a way that the town found itself passed by, a turn-off community easily missed at fifty-five miles per hour. And for one reason or another, I kept missing it for eleven years. Then, one bright bicentennial June afternoon, I braked at the exit ramp and turned into town.

Main Street was deserted except for an old man who was taking the sun on the front steps of the Phoenicia Hotel. I said hello and went past him and reached for the remembered brass handle of the door. "No you don't," said the old man. "They're closed."

I noticed then that the blinds were drawn behind the front windows. "Owners on vacation?" I asked.

"Nope," said the man on the steps. "Just away."

"For how long?"

"Well," said the man, "the way I figure it, for a helluva long time."

Across the street, Richard Ricciardella was polishing glasses behind the bar of the restaurant his father had opened with high hopes in the flush years of the early sixties. The hotel had indeed closed, he said. And a few other places he wouldn't mention were on the edge. It had not been a good year. I asked him how he accounted for the decline.

"The gasoline shortage in seventy-four didn't help us any," said Ricciardella. "But that wasn't the beginning. Even before then, people just started coming up less. Used to be they'd arrive Friday night and not go home to the city till after Sunday dinner. Now you see the day-trippers with their thermoses and sandwich bags. The skiers don't bother to stop anymore. Coming or going, they drive straight through. I'll tell you. It's a different kind of place around here. Makes you think about moving on to where the action is."

Action of the sort desired by the Ricciardellas of Phoenicia is hard to find in the Catskills these days. Here and there along the major thoroughfares a few oases of summer pleasure linger on, and of winter pleasure, too. Hunter projects a healthy economic image, as do Liberty and Monticello to the south. In a few scattered places, according to one report, tourism actually increased in the recessional 1970s. Greene and Sullivan counties still look to the resort industry for their economic life-blood. And in the larger region defined by the Catskill Study Commission's thin green line, resorts are said to account for some twenty thousand full- and part-time jobs, $100 million in annual payrolls, and $11 million in property taxes, which is not to be sniffed at. Still, tourism in the mountains is not what it used to be. Or what it could be. Between 1954 and 1973, the region experienced a net loss of 420 hotels and boardinghouses. Red ink in the ledgers, and the owners gone away for a helluva long time. The village of Fleischmanns, up Route 28 from Phoenicia and once the most glittering spa on the old Ulster and Delaware line, could count fifty hotels in the years before World War II. The last time I looked, only four remained standing.

Hard times in Phoenicia and Fleischmanns no doubt reflect a number of factors that have reshaped the pattern of recreation in American life. As any pop sociologist will be happy to explain, the primary villains in this postwar scenario were the automobile and the suburb. The automobile brought highways (some say the highways brought automobiles) and mobility. And while mobility meant one could drive to the Catskills quickly, it also meant one could leave just as fast. And it meant that one could go farther afield. In Roscoe, there was great rejoicing among entrepreneurs when a four-lane Quickway replaced the two-lane "Old Twisty" Route 17. The new highway was quick, all right. It sped New Yorkers right through Sullivan County to the Finger Lakes beyond Binghamton. And now Roscoe, too, is passed by, like Phoenicia. As for the suburban phenomenon and its effect on leisure trends, there are innumerable theories; one is that with green grass and trees and a wading pool in the backyard, who needs South Lake and the Pine Orchard? This particular premise, however, begins to unravel in the face of a more recent phenomenon—the second home. Apparently the salubrious air of suburbia is no longer enough. "The Great American Dream today is the weekend retreat," says Ulster County Planning Director Herbert Hekler. "It's an old farm with acreage or a cabin in the woods." Some Catskill businessmen are resentful of the new weekenders. "I guess they pay taxes," a Sullivan County innkeeper complains. "But they don't do *us* any good. They never eat out or go out. Why, they won't even buy their groceries up here. They bring 'em."

Shifting trends in public taste and transportation have tormented the proprietors of the region's resorts since the bonanza years of Charles Beach's Catskill Mountain House. Beach had resisted the onslaught of the railroads in the 1870s. A decade later he was embracing them out of competitive necessity. And the competition was formidable. Just a mile or so south of the Mountain House stood the towering Kaaterskill Hotel, the epitome of luxury and elegance and the preferred resort of such notable sometime guests as Oscar Wilde and Ulysses Grant. The Kaaterskill, in fact, was the direct result of a rather specific shift in taste, namely, that of one George Harding, who for many years had been one of Beach's regular boarders. Perhaps Harding had been too regular, for one night at supper, weary of the Mountain House's monotonous fare and concerned for his daughter's diet, Harding demanded a special order of fried chicken. The waiter refused. Charles Beach refused, and sternly suggested to George Harding that if he didn't approve of the Mountain House menu he could jolly well take his daughter and his business elsewhere. Which, in a manner of speaking, is exactly what Harding did. The Harding-built Kaaterskill opened two summers later; and though it failed to outlive its landmark neighbor, its fashionable amenities overshadowed those of the Beach resort for thirty years.

The era of the great Catskill hotels—the "Gilded Age" as some historians prefer to call it—lasted until World War I. In that time, the famous and fashionable would flock to such summer palaces as the Laurel House at Kaaterskill Falls, the Overlook House near Woodstock, the Grand Hotel at Monka Hill in Highmount, the Tremper House, and, at Stamford, the Rexmere and Churchill Hall. Both Beach and Harding died in 1902, too early to preside over the decline and fall of their respective establishments. In 1918, the Otis Elevating Railroad shut down. In 1924, the Kaaterskill Hotel burned to the ground. So did the Overlook House, two years later. In 1942, the Catskill Mountain House celebrated its 119th—and final—season, then settled down in the Pine Orchard for a long-time dying. In 1952, passenger service was terminated on the New York, Ontario & Western Railway through Sullivan County. The Ulster and Delaware held out for two more years. In 1963, the ragged, hollow, vandalized shell of the Mountain House was razed by the New York State Conservation Department, which had acquired the property. Four years later the state put its torch to the Laurel House as well. Of all the truly great resort hotels of the Gilded Age, only one remains, the Rexmere at Stamford. In recent years, it has served nobly as a seminary, an office complex, and, for a time, as headquarters of the Temporary State Commission to Study the Catskills. So it goes. *Requiescat in internal combustion, amen.*

Throughout the rise and fall of the gilded hotels, accommodations of more modest dimension were helping to shape the region's future dependence on tourism. As early as the 1830s, country inns and boardinghouses were catering to the needs of hardy urban gentlemen who preferred hunting and angling to poetry and parasols. Along the streams of Ulster, Delaware, and Greene counties, scores of unpretentious hostels sprang up. The Ontario & Western ran fishermen's specials into Sullivan County, where fly-casting disciples of Theodore Gordon had discovered the glories of the Willowemoc, the Beaverkill, and the Neversink. White Lake, west of Monticello, got its start as a summer resort on the basis of a widely circulated rumor: White Lake had yielded the largest trout ever netted in America.

One did not have to hunt or fish to take advantage of the lower rates at the boardinghouses. As paid vacations became more common, working-class people from the cities rode the rails to the mountains to pick wild berries and drink fresh milk. Catskill farmers converted their houses to accommodate the overflow from established hotels. Many discovered that changing the bed linen was not only easier but far more profitable than milking the cows. In the world of the boardinghouse, the pleasures of summer were gayer and freer than they were in the prim milieu that prevailed at the grand hotels. Gamblers and flimflam men began to appear in the mountains. Gypsies raced horses and gazed into their crystal balls. Indians were imported from Canada to ply their trinkets on the porches of resorts. Italians arrived with musical boxes and dancing monkeys. German Protestants and German Jews began to congregate in the boardinghouses of Tannersville and Livingston Manor. Hearing a babel of alien languages, the summer gentry from New York and Charleston retreated behind the high iron gates of their private parks. At Roxbury, the son of raiload magnate Jay Gould assembled a vast estate that included a game preserve for elk. At Griffin's Corners, Charles Fleischmann, the Ohio yeast manufacturer, installed his family in an elegant compound and hired professional ballplayers to perform on his own baseball diamond.

In Sullivan County, meanwhile, the resort business was booming. Orthodox Jews in flight from the sweatshops of Manhattan's Lower East Side were flocking to the boardinghouses and hotels clustered along the Ontario & Western and throughout the hills near Woodridge and Fallsburgh. Romance had nothing to do with it. The Jews of New York were realists. Let the Gentiles scribble poetry in the Pine Orchard; the Jews would create a world of Yiddish theater at Lake Kiamesha. Let Fleischmann (a Hungarian Jew himself) import baseball players to

86

Griffin's Corners; Monticello and Liberty would import actors from Broadway. Would send actors *to* Broadway. In time, the southern Catskills would be advertising big-name entertainers at the Nevelle, the Concord, Kutsher's, and Grossinger's. Danny Kaye and Milton Berle and Red Buttons would come home again to Sullivan County. And the very last of the great resorts would linger on into the 1970s—by the grace of large conventions and the high cost of a European vacation.

Fred Haas is the proprietor of the Edgewood Hotel in Livingston Manor and he is much indebted to the French. Haas himself is of German descent. "Bless the French," he was saying one day over lunch in his dining room. "When it costs you a dollar fifty for a cup of coffee in Paris, how can we lose?" Haas claims he cannot. "If the prices weren't so high in Europe," he was saying, "a quarter of the people you see here today would be over there right now. So look where they are. Right here. It's been a very good year."

Like many owners of old-time resorts in the southern Catskills (the Edgewood dates to 1916), Haas believes that when the squeeze is on, business reverts to established places. "It's the way with people," he says. "People will go to where people are." But the people who go to the Edgewood are mostly people who have been there before. Mostly people over forty. Mostly people who are content with three solid meals and a comfortable bed and a day of quiet planned activities, with a Barbra Streisand movie held in reserve in the event of rain. One looks around the dining room, the common room, the visible precincts of the 600-acre grounds and wonders: Where are the young? Surely not in Europe. And one also wonders what will become of the Edgewood and the other quiet places like it when the people who are mostly over forty are mostly over sixty or seventy, and then gone. As Haas was saying, people go to where people are. Or as Elaine Grossinger Etess of Grossinger's was saying: "Fresh air, fine scenery, and good food are no longer enough."

In 1974, at Fleischmanns, the aging Funcrest Hotel was destroyed by fire. The event was routinely reported by the local press, fires of unknown origin being old news, especially those involving hotels that were over the hill. The *Fleischmanns Flyer* nevertheless used the occasion to comment editorially on the trend of things in the Catskills. "One by one," the *Flyer* noted, "the great hotels have gone lighting a mountain night with an eerie glow." And it added:

> But the Catskills have a strange way of covering every grand scheme with second growth timber. The tanneries, the mountainside farms, the bluestone quarries, the wood-turning industry, the grand hotels. Each in its turn has blossomed, spinned top profits off for owners from elsewhere, and vanished under new deciduous growth.

The forest. In the Catskills, everything keeps coming back to that.

Grand Gorge United Methodist Church

Farm in Treadwell

Deserted farmhouse

Ruins of Overlook Mountain House

Prattsville tombstone

Forest and Stream

A town is saved, not more by the righteous men in it than by the woods and swamps that surround it.

—Henry David Thoreau,
"Excursions"

Balsam Lake Mountain rises between the headwaters of Mill Brook and the Beaverkill River in Ulster County. It is said to be seventeenth in order of height among Catskill peaks, a distinction that serves scant justice on the view from its summit. The view is extraordinary, for Balsam Lake Mountain probably stands closer to the region's geographic center than any other promontory about three thousand feet. On a clear day, from the fire tower, one can turn a full 360 degrees and see more of the Catskill Forest Preserve than from almost any other vantage point save the top of Slide Mountain. Here and there on the distant slopes are a few open patches, the fields and pastures of hideaway farms tucked deep, out of sight, in the valleys. Villages and roads are likewise hidden by intervening ridgetops, as are the great reservoirs of Pepacton on the west and Ashokan to the east. So it is mostly forest that one sees from Balsam Lake Mountain—acres and leagues of it, stretching in every direction, a terrestial ocean lapping at the shores of the azure sky.

Not everyone who comes to the top of this mountain is pleased with the view. Most are. No doubt most are city-folk hikers who would be furious if it were otherwise. To them, the Catskill Forest Preserve is a sacred resource, best left unpatched; a place where trees are permitted to die of old age instead of by amputation; a refuge from the pressures of urban living. Some country folk see it differently. To them, the preserve is a wasteland where trees are permitted to rot on the stump and deer are found starving for lack of adequate browse. They feel certain pressures, too; namely, the pressures of earning a country living in a region where forests cover more than 60 pecent of the land yet provide a base for only 2 percent of the total employment.

A battle between those who would keep the forest forever wild and those who would open it to commercial uses has been raging in the Catskills almost since the State Forest Preserve was established in 1885. Originally, the idea of creating such a preserve had arisen from an effort to save the Adirondack forests from the kind of logging practices that were then laying waste to the pine woods of Michigan and upper New York. The harmful effects of siltation had just been discovered. People downstate were fearful. If the loggers were allowed a free hand in the Adirondacks, it was said, silt would wash down the Hudson River and choke both the Erie Canal and New York Harbor. The state's economic well-being therefore demanded protection for the Adirondacks. The Catskills were an afterthought—after it was ascertained that New York City would run out of drinking water unless it soon tapped a new source of supply. The officials who were paid to worry about such things naturally looked to the Catskills. Water there was not only pure but plentiful (not to mention the fact that the salubrious effects of forested watersheds had just been discovered). Thus did New York State mandate a forest preserve for both mountain regions.

Curiously, the initial legislation failed to prohibit the sale or cutting of timber. This provided a loophole in the protective mechanism large enough to encourage abuses. In 1895, Article XIV of the state constitution closed that loophole by providing not only that the preserve shall be "forever kept as wild forest lands," but that the lands "shall not be leased, sold or exchanged, or be taken by any corporation, public or private, nor shall the timber thereon be sold, removed or destroyed." Over the years, various proposals have been advanced to amend Article XIV in a manner calculated to accommodate special concessions and commercial enterprises. The debate in the Catskills has centered primarily on the management—or mismanagement, as some critics would have it—of the Forest Preserve's untapped timber resources.

The preserve, of course, represents only a fraction of the region's total forest resource. In fact, more than 85 percent of the forest land within the Study Commission's green line is privately owned. In the four core Catskill counties of Greene, Delaware, Sullivan, and Ulster, for example, 1.5 million acres are classified as commercial forest land producing or capable of producing wood products. In contrast, the Forest Preserve encompasses only 250,000 acres, an area one-sixth the size of the commercial forest. The privately owned woodlands contain an estimated 4.6 billion board feet of timber; the Forest Preserve, .6 billion board feet. It could therefore be said of the Catskills that one cannot see the forest for all the trees.

Among certain long-time residents of the region, the "forever wild" principle is about as popular as the Old-World notion of taxation without representation. "No one wants to desecrate the woods," says one bitter critic of the forever wild concept, "but the amount of mature timber that tumbles down in the preserve and rots is a crime. I can understand why they went ahead with such stringent controls in the 1880s. But it's almost a hundred years later. It's an insult to the professional forester to have to administer this kind of law." And a Roscoe observer complains: "The wood's just going to waste. I say, let the people cut it. If it took fifty of them off welfare, it would help, wouldn't it?"

Demands that the Forest Preserve be opened to logging to regenerate the region's economy tend to obscure how little economic activity there has been of late in the private woodlands. The annual harvest within the green-line region has averaged about 75 million board feet—not much, considering what is available for a sustained yield. What is more, a good part of the saw logs harvested goes to mills and finishing plants outside the Catskill region. The portion that remains for local processing is barely enough to sustain two or three medium-size mills, two score smaller ones, a work force of 1700 and an annual payroll of $13 million. "A strong forest products industry could provide a significant economic base for the Catskills without ever touching the Forest Preserve," says Paul Keller, regional forester for the State Department of Environmental Conservation. "But right now, too many things are militating against it."

By most accounts, the greatest deterrent to a revitalized forest industry in the Catskills is the checkerboard pattern of land ownership resulting from a proliferation of second homes. The "little cabin" tucked away in the woods is no longer the quaint phenomenon it used to be. In some sections of the Catskills, second homes for urban refugees have risen at every bend of a back-country road, and the timber surrounding the homes is not for sale. Pollsters report that many owners of small woodland properties harbor negative feelings about timber production. They do not want loggers making a mess of their woods. They want peace and quiet, and trees dying of old age. The amount of timber land-owners of this persuasion have effectively withdrawn from the potential saw-log pool would be difficult to ascertain; but no doubt it is considerable. Resident owners of larger holdings, on the other hand, are occasionally too eager to invite the loggers to their woods. Taxation weighs heavily on them. When the tax bills come due, the whine of the chain saw can be heard from the back forties of old estates and tumble-down farms. Overcutting has already occurred on a number of larger land-holdings. On others, the owners have been unable to afford the out-of-pocket expense of such management practices as thinning and fertilization. As a result, their third-growth timber is of pole size. Few mills in the Catskills are equipped to handle such small logs.

Other factors are aligned against the region's forest industry, not the least of which is New York State's high workman's compensation rates. The rate for loggers is nearly $20 per $100 of wages earned. There are certain administrative problems as well. The Forest Practices Act, administered by the Department of Environmental Conservation, offers a free consulting service to private wood-lot owners (the marking of saw timber, guidance in obtaining buyers); yet the state foresters responsible for the program are already overwhelmed with their own management problems, especially the problem of policing recreational use of the Forest Preserve. The department's efficiency is further fragmented by jurisdictions that ignore the regional integrity of the Catskills and the Forest Preserve. Ulster and Sullivan counties fall within the jurisdiction of the department's regional office in New Paltz, which also covers Orange, Rockland, and Westchester counties downstate. Greene and Delaware counties, in matters of forestry, are administered by separate district offices in Catskill and Stamford. The lines of communication between these offices are said to be thin. There is no cohesive policy for managing the region's forests.

There *could* be, and one devoutly hopes some day there will be. Given its proximity to the vast market place of the New York metropolitan area, given a cohesive management policy and the manpower to administer it, given new tax incentives to encourage sustained production on viable timberlands, and investors capable of supporting new secondary wood processing and furniture manufacturing plants, a strong forest industry could indeed be established in the Catskills—without, as Paul Keller sees it, ever putting the saw blade to the forever wild stands of the State Forest Preserve.

The other great renewable resource of the Catskills is water. From every ridge and mountainside it seeps, trickling over mossy ledges, swirling in shaded pools, rushing down to the valleys in freshets, rolling along the ancient streambeds to the Mohawk, the Hudson, the Delaware, the Susquehanna, and the sea. On its way, however, a portion of the flow of every major Catskill watershed save the Beaverkill-Willowemoc is impounded in one or another of six reservoirs, then dispatched by gravity tunnel to the pipes and faucets of New York City. Every day, nearly one and a half billion gallons of Catskill water—about ninety percent of the city's needs—gurgle down the municipal drain. As if this were not enough, the city's water managers from time to time trot out new schemes to squeeze even more from the mountains. Yet already, according to one state report, the region's water resources "have been developed to a point of near exhaustion."

New York City has been looking upstate for its water supplies since 1837, when it purchased rights along the Croton River in Westchester County. The Croton system sufficed until the turn of the century. Then an extended drought compelled the city to search further afield. In the Ramapo Mountains of Orange County, speculators anticipating the city's shortage had already acquired the water rights and were offering them at exorbitant prices. This forced the city to consider tapping the streams of the Catskills. There was litigation in the courts. The mountain people were not about to allow New York City to siphon off their water. But the courts ruled they had to, basing the decision on the right of eminent domain. In 1917, water began rising behind the city's brand-new bluestone dam at Olive Bridge on Esopus Creek. It would continue rising until the 10,000-acre Ashokan Reservoir was filled to an average depth of fifty feet. Seven villages and 2600 graves had to be relocated in deference to 132 billion gallons of water. A 92-mile aqueduct, tunneling under the Rondout Valley, the Shawangunks, and the Hudson River (at a depth of 1000 feet), carried the Esopus water to Kensico Reservoir in Westchester County. And this was only for openers.

The second stage of the Catskill system was completed in 1927. At Gilboa on Schoharie Creek, another dam backed up the waters of that stream almost to Prattsville; and the Shandaken Tunnel carried the water south (backwards, if you will) to Esopus Creek at Allaben, some twelve miles upstream from Ashokan Reservoir. But the Schoharie had hardly met the Esopus when the city water planners realized that this would not fully satiate the growing metropolitan thirst. And so—on to the Delaware watershed, with a reservoir on the Neversink, another on Rondout Creek, and a third on the East Branch (Pepacton). Construction was completed in 1955. The Pepacton Reservoir is connected to the Rondout by a 25-mile tunnel; the Neversink to the Rondout by a 5-mile tunnel; and Rondout to New York City by the 85-mile Delaware Aqueduct, which generally releases its water into Kensico Reservoir, so that Neversink can meet Croton, Croton can meet Pepacton, and all three can meet Schoharie-Esopus. Last but not least into the receiving line was the West Branch of the Delaware, which arrived at Kensico in

1967 by way of the Cannonsville Reservoir at Deposit, and by tunnel to Rondout. And all of these mingled waters flow on to the spigots of a city that has yet to implement any significant conservation measures, to mandate universal metering, or, for that matter, to fix its leaks. "I've been down to friends' apartments in the city," says Art Flick of West Kill. "And almost every time I find the same leaky faucet that was dribbling away our water two years ago."

The city's reservoirs are both an asset and a liability to the people of the Catskills. The assets accrue largely to the towns in which the dams are located, for under New York State law, the reservoirs and ancillary water-supply properties are fully taxable. Such towns as Colchester, Gilboa, Neversink, and Olive therefore look to the city for more than 70 percent of their local tax payments. Still, there is some dispute as to whether these taxes are fair compensation for the loss of productive river-bottom farmland, or for the physical dissection of a town such as Andes, split in halves by the Pepacton Reservoir.

In recent years, local disenchantment with the city's reservoirs has centered largely on the issue of water releases. For its part, the city historically has sought to maintain the reservoirs at peak capacity—a fine idea for storing water, but with occasional horrid effects on farms and fisheries downstream. In the spring, high runoffs can result in floods; in the late summer and fall, low flows are insufficient to sustain downstream irrigation and fishery resources. The operation of the Shandaken Tunnel, for example, has been described by a state commission as "capricious." Sudden opening or closing of the tunnel has caused extreme fluctuations in the water level of Esopus Creek. The flow from the tunnel is frequently turbid. High water has destroyed trout habitat. Low water has left fish to die and rot in stagnant pools. "They just about ruined the fishing," says Art Flick, an expert on trout-stream ecology. "We've seen some very bad fish kills. One time the water temperature rose to ninety degrees in the main stem of the Delaware. In the East Branch, below Pepacton, the water got so low last year it smelled." But conditions in the streams may be improving. In 1976, the state imposed on New York City new regulations governing the release of reservoir waters for downstream uses. "If they handle these regulations wisely," says Flick, "we have every expectation we'll have the best fishing in the east right here in the Catskills. There's a tremendous amount of natural reproduction in these streams. All they need is a natural flow of water."

Aside from the issue of water releases, the reservoirs raise another question in the minds of those who are concerned with a fuller use of the region's resources. And the question is: Can and should the reservoirs' recreational potential be developed? The dominant answer seems to be yes, though one hears strong dissents from New York City officials as well as from Catskill folk who reside in some of the reservoir towns.

For all of their brooks and streams, the Catskills are conspicuously short on "flat" water. There are a few small lakes in Sullivan County; but for the most part, aside from the city's reservoirs, the Catskills do not have the kind of standing water that Americans seem to demand these days to satisfy their love affair with boats and beaches. In fact, because of nature's failure to supply the Catskills with lakes, many vacationing travelers pass the region by on their way to bigger waters, as in the Adirondacks. The reservoirs, of course, are surely big enough, and beautiful enough. But, because of the city's fastidious concern for the purity of its drinking water, they are not accessible to the public. The only use the city will tolerate is fishing, by permit only, in rowboats that for some arcane and incomprehensible reason cannot be moved from one reservoir to another. And no picnicking. And no hiking in the surrounding woods. And no skating on the ice in the winter. "Don't test them," says Ulster County Planning Director Herbert Hekler of the city's water managers. "You show up at Ashokan Reservoir without a permit and a fishing rod and they'll arrest you."

Such restrictive management of water-supply lands is common throughout the Northeast, where nineteenth-century attitudes seem to linger a bit longer than elsewhere in the nation. Elsewhere, municipalities generally allow a wider range of recreational activities on and around their reservoirs, including, in several western instances, swimming. After all, is bait fishing from a leaky rowboat any more compatible with pure water than sailing or canoeing? Most public health officials doubt it. Indeed, except for the intransigence of the municipal bureaucracy, there appears to be no valid reason whatsoever why the city reservoirs and their adjacent uplands cannot be opened to public use under appropriate controls and in accordance with a comprehensive plan that would take into account both the environmental and economic impact of more liberal recreational policies on adjacent communities and the region as a whole. Nonmotorized boating, ice skating, ice fishing, picnicking, and camping are wholly compatible with the water-supply function. As the President's Council on Environmental Quality has noted, it is no longer possible or desirable "to reserve whole watersheds simply for the production of drinking water—there are too many competing demands on the land near urban areas. . . ."

Prospects

We can use our scientific knowledge to poison the air, corrupt the waters, blacken the face of the country, and harass our souls with loud and discordant noises, or we can mitigate and abolish all these things.

—JOHN BURROUGHS,
Summit of the Years

West a few miles from the village of Roxbury, on a slope overlooking a side valley of the East Branch of the Delaware River, is the grave of John Burroughs, the Catskill writer who believed that the wealth of the universe was waiting at everyone's door. In his time, which lasted from 1837 to 1921, Burroughs's universe was rich indeed; and he shared its wonders in hundreds of essays on nature and the simple things that often count most in life. As a young man, before the flowing beard turned white and the strength went out of the writing hand, Burroughs developed a strong attachment to the Catskills. "Those hills," he wrote, "comfort me as no other place in the world does. It is home there." Like his friend and contemporary John Muir, afoot in the High Sierra, Burroughs wandered alone through the mountains of his eastern homeland, cherishing the solitude, the wildness, the company of bumblebees and chipmunks. He especially cherished a good view. One of his favorites was from a large, flat-top boulder in the field behind Woodchuck Lodge, his summer home. This is where Burroughs was buried, beside the boulder he fondly called Boyhood Rock. It is said that he spent many an hour there, wondering what the world was made of.

The view from Boyhood Rock today could not be much different from the perspective that Burroughs enjoyed; but the world, whatever it is made of, has changed. And the old man had sensed some of the changes coming, for he had warned of the noises that harass the soul, of corruptions that blacken the face of the country. Burroughs had seen the Catskills abused in his own time. He had contemplated the scars left behind by the tanners and quarriers and acid-wood people. He had expressed the hope that humankind would somehow learn to "mitigate and abolish" such wounds. No doubt John Burroughs worried a good deal about the future of the Catskills. In that respect, were he alive today he would not be alone.

Of late, there has been much concern about the future of the Catskills. In 1971 the state legislature passed, and the then governor, Nelson Rockefeller, signed into law a bill creating a Temporary State Commission to Study the Catskills. The measure authorized the commission to:

> . . . make a study of the Catskill Region which shall include, but not be limited to, the conservation and development of the natural resources of the region, notably, the flora, fauna, scenic beauty and environmental purity; the strengthening of cultural resources, social organizations, economy and general well-being of the rural communities and the development of measures by which the region may draw strength from neighboring cities, but at the same time protecting itself from unplanned population growth. Also studied should be the necessity of strengthening policy regarding management, acquisition and use of public land; the development of controls for highways, public buildings and utilities; increased recreational facilities including the feasibility of greater use of water supply reservoirs; the measures to be taken by local governments to assure that the development of private lands is consistent with long-range plans.

The commission's work got under way in the spring of 1973. Its final report was rendered two years later. In the interim, commissioners and staff members met with 450 civic organizations, advisory panels, and local government officials; held some 30 public hearings; and issued about two dozen technical reports on various aspects of the study.

For the most part, the commission's findings were far from encouraging. The regional economy was a shambles. Unemployment was running twenty to fifty percent above the statewide average. Personal and median family income were well below the upstate levels. Manufacturing was showing no signs of growth. Although farm income was increasing, the number of farms was declining. In six years, 200,000 acres had been withdrawn from agriculture—a loss of 17 percent.

Throughout the region, the commission noted, "ill-considered, haphazard and hasty development has taken its toll from seller and buyer alike. Improper land use has resulted in sewage, water, and other problems; and has depreciated investment. . . . Local communities are paying their price in additional, and often unanticipated, public services. . . ." Planning for the future, said the commission with some measure of understatement, "is in need of improvement."

In an interim report that inventoried the region's planning activities as of the fall of 1973, the commission had found that of some 160 cities, towns, and villages, 40 were without planning boards. Many of those that were said to exist "met so infrequently that they were planning boards in name only and were without accomplishment." The commission further noted that only 61 of the 160 communities "were making use of subdivision regulations or zoning ordinances, or both." Four years later more than half still had no subdivision or zoning controls.

For lack of local land-use controls, the Catskill Region in recent years has witnessed a number of environmental outrages: new construction in floodplain areas, septic fields discharging wastes into adjacent streams, the ubiquitous mobile home plunked down in any convenient vacant lot, gaudy strip development along such highways as Routes 28 and 23A. "In some places," says one planner, "the Catskills are beginning to approach the social and visual cacophony of Appalachia." An alarmed Davenport resident warns that "our hillsides are starting to look like the squatters' tin slums in South American cities." Echoes of John Burroughs's "loud and discordant noises."

Resistance to planning runs deep in the mountains. Many indi-

108

viduals view the town planner, if there is one, as a threat to private property rights. The town planner sees the county planner as a threat to home rule. And the county planner sees the regional planner as a threat to county autonomy. Some dedicated local officials despair at all the feuding. "Sullivan County is fighting Ulster County, and Ulster County is fighting Delaware County and no one is standing up to speak for the Catskills," says one local official. And environmental attorney David Sive, a Mill Brook property owner, wonders: "Does the water roll in two different directions when it hits the town or county line?"

Some people apparently think it should. In Leeds in the late winter of 1977, the New York State Assembly Committee on Environmental Conservation conducted the first of a series of public hearings on measures proposing creation of a Catskill Regional Resources Management Commission, a permanent agency that would implement some of the defunct study commission's recommendations and try to establish a measure of balance between the goals of environmental quality and economic development. About four hundred Catskill residents turned up at the hearing. If the volume of catcalls, booing, and applause can be taken as any indicator, most of those present opposed the creation of such an agency. (Several years earlier, however, an opinion survey commissioned by the study group found that sixty-six percent of the region's people felt that inadequate land-use planning was a significant problem in their communities.) At Leeds, an official from Hunter spoke passionately of the importance of "home rule." The man from the Farm Bureau said he feared a usurpation of property rights. And the speaker from the conservative Constitutional Rights Association announced that land-use controls were "absurd." The people of the Catskills, he said, "can survive without these plans. Land-use control is people control. Please leave us alone." Sherret Chase, president of the nonprofit Catskill Center for Conservation and Development, had anticipated just such an appeal. It was a feeling, he said, that one could sympathize with. Nevertheless, warned Chase, "isolationism is as costly as it is impractical. The greatest danger facing some parts of the Catskills, particularly those most economically depressed, is that state and federal government will accede to the wishes of the antiplanners and leave us alone—all alone."

David Loeks of New Paltz is a regional planner and president of Mid-Hudson Pattern for Progress. Like many planners whose fingers have been scorched in the fires of home-rule discontent, he is a gradualist who believes that all good things come in time, if one has patience. We were talking one day about the problems of the Catskills. An effort to extend the life of the temporary study commission had just been defeated in the New York Assembly. Would there ever be an end to the grass-roots provincialism, I wondered? Could a spirit of true regionalism, a larger sense of place, ever take root in the mountains? Loeks shrugged the questions aside. "If at first you don't succeed," he said, "quit. But only for a little while. Because yesterday's heresy is tomorrow's cliché."

And what exactly might tomorrow's cliché for the Catskill region be like? Will the wealth of the universe be waiting at its door, or will its soul be harassed by discordant noises? A bit of both, I suspect. In any event, the planning process no doubt will come to the mountains—in time, and with the grudging consent of those who wish to be left alone. People will begin to understand that the regulation of land use is not a taking of property but rather a protection of basic human rights.

"The question of planning and controls for the Catskills," reflects Herb Field of the *Daily Mail* in Catskill, "is a question of devising a code of rules on which most can agree, and all must abide, in order to protect the region for the benefit and enjoyment of its inhabitants and visitors, for now and in the future."

Writing in 1973, Peter Borrelli, executive director of the Catskill Center and a young veteran of environmental conflicts from Maine to Florida, described "the Catskills of tomorrow" as "a regional community and landscape with a strong sense of place, where the needs of man are in harmony with nature." As rational decisions are applied to the land, I suspect there could be a concomitant improvement in the region's economy. Tax reform, for example—the assessing of land on the basis of current use rather than potential use—could preserve the integrity of the small farm. Commerce and industry might well be attracted to places where development does not diminish an essentially rural environment. Tourism would surely benefit where clutter and sprawl are ruled out. Utopia? Why not? As Oscar Wilde noted, "A map of the world that does not include Utopia is not worth even glancing at, for it leaves out the one country at which Humanity is always landing. And when Humanity lands there, it looks out, and seeing a better country, sets sail. Progress is the realization of Utopias."

There is one special place in the Catskills that keeps calling me back. It is not quite Utopia, but in one respect it is like Utopia: It does not appear on any map. If it did, I expect that the place would no longer be special. Not for me, anyway. I have been there half a dozen times. It is a quiet stretch of creek bottom, about a quarter-mile long, with a stand of second-growth hemlock leaning over the stream and a fine polished boulder for perching. The boulder sits high and dry most of the year. In the spring, with the freshets coming off the mountainsides, the stream rises and you have to wet your ankles to get there. Not a very big boulder, this one. Not like Burroughs's Boyhood Rock. This one is just about right for one person at a time. The top slopes in such a way that one is best situated facing downstream, toward the hemlocks. In the late afternoon, one can see the water gliding darkly in shadow under the feathered branches. Trout sometimes lurk in that pool. Though I have never been able to dredge up the evidence, I have seen others do it. Most notably by the old man with the wading staff, who believes in the power of the new moon.

The old man was working his way upstream one afternoon, holding to the center of the creek and making short casts to either side with a long cane pole. He was floating night crawlers on an unweighted line. A heavy wading staff was strapped to his free wrist and he leaned on it between casts to steady his progress in the swift current. A wicker creel on his hip appeared to be his only other piece of equipment. I watched him move abreast of the hemlocks. Only an hour earlier, I had worked that pool myself without so much as a single strike. Now the old man dropped his night crawler at the head of the glide, and before it was halfway into the pool he was playing a fine fish.

"That was nice work down there," I said to the old man when

he came ashore below my rock. "I was beginning to think there aren't any trout in this creek."

"There's still a few," he said. "Not like it used to be, though. And not as big as they used to be either."

We talked for a while then as the sun went down behind the mountains. The old man said he had been fishing this creek for thirty years, and others—"from the Bushkill to the Beaverkill"—for half a century. He said he figured he ought to know where every trout in the Catskills lies. "But there's some days," he allowed, "when you're just as well not bothering to go out." I asked him if there was any way of knowing that in advance.

"Oh, sure," he said. "It's the new moon that counts every time. Three days before, the day of the new moon, and three days after. That gives you a week with the hungry trout. After that—phooey."

I hadn't been keeping track of the moon recently, so I asked the old man where we stood in relation to that one good week with the hungry trout. He replied that it was finished, that today would be the last productive day for three weeks. "It's the same with people," he added. "We are kin with the fish. What affects the fish affects all of us. You watch that the next time a new moon is up. You will rise to a fine cast. You'll see."

No doubt the old man's optimism had something to do with the trout in his creel. He had had a good day in the water. He could afford to be hopeful. I asked him how he felt about the future of the mountains. Would they change for better or for worse in the coming years?

"Well," he said, "that's a hard one to figure. You get too many people crowding in around here and the mountains are ruined for sure. You get too many people moving out and that's no good either. I like to think we'll see something in between." The old man raised his cane pole above the water and sent a shiver along it with a flick of his wrist. "It's like this trout pole here," he said. "A thing don't work unless it's balanced. You believe that?"

Yes, I believed it, all right. And for the sake of the Catskill Mountains, I said I hoped that everyone else did, too.

Peck Hollow Brook

< Panther Mountain from Slide Mountain

Balsam Lake

Southern view from Balsam Lake Mountain

Tunis Pond, Hardenburgh

Headwaters of Beaverkill

Kaaterskill Falls

Esopus Creek and Wittenberg Mountain

Hudson River >

Pepacton Reservoir *(overleaf)* >

North and South Lake *(last page)* >>

Beaver pond near Stony Clove